Our health, our care, our say:

a new direction for community services

Presented to Parliament
by the Secretary of State for Health
by Command of Her Majesty

January 2006

Cm 6737

£26.00

P

Contents

Introduction 1

Foreword 3

Executive summary 5
Reforming health and social care 5
The context of the White Paper 6
What the White Paper will achieve 6
The White Paper is aiming to achieve four main goals 7
How are we going to achieve these improvements? 8
Conclusions 10

1. Our ambition for community-based care 11
Our vision 13
Listening to people 14
Our challenge 16
A new strategic direction 17
Making our vision a reality 18
Well-being in our communities 19
Resources 21
Our proposals 21
References 21

2. Enabling health, independence and well-being 23
Introduction 25
Helping people to look after their own health and well-being 31
Shifting the system towards prevention 46
Social prescribing 51
National leadership 51
References 52

3. Better access to general practice 55
Introduction 57
Making it easier to register with an open practice 59
Tackling closed lists 60
Making it easier for responsive practices to expand 61
Health inequalities 63
Making it easier to get care at the right time 69
Ensuring practices are open when the public wants 70
Choosing **your** primary care professional 73
Choosing services that reflect your needs 74
References 74

4.   Better access to community services   **77**

Introduction   79
Giving people more choice and control over their care services   81
Community health services   87
Making better use of community pharmacy services   87
Improving urgent access   88
Rapid access to sexual health services   91
Rapid access to mental health services   92
Screening for cancer   93
Access to allied health professionals' therapy services   94
Reaching out to people in need   95
Expectant mothers   96
Improving immunisation services   98
Teenagers   99
People with learning disabilities   100
Access to health services for offenders   102
Older people   103
End-of-life care   103
References   104

5.   Support for people with longer-term needs   **107**

Introduction   109
The strategic challenge   109
Helping people take control   112
Better assessment and care planning   114
Pointing the way to the future   118
References   125

6.   Care closer to home   **127**

The need for change   129
Specialist care more locally   129
Shifting resources   139
Community facilities accessible to all   143
Incentives and commissioning   152
References   154

7.   Ensuring our reforms put people in control   **155**

Introduction   157
Services that engage citizens and respond to their concerns   157
Effective commissioning   161
Providing support through a national commissioning framework   166
Commissioning responsive services   169
References   176

8.   Making sure change happens   **177**
        Introduction   179
        High-quality information   179
        Guaranteeing quality   182
        Assessment of quality   183
        Regulation   184
        Patient safety   185
        Developing the workforce   185
        Working across boundaries   185
        References   189

9.   A timetable for action   **191**
        Introduction   192
        Key implementation tasks and timings by commitment   193

Annex A: The consultation and the listening exercise: the main messages   197
        Better health, independence and well-being   199
        More responsive services with fast and convenient access   200
        Better support for people with the greatest need to continue
            to live more independently   200
        More services available closer to home and in the community   201

Annex B: Independence, Well-being and Choice   **203**
        Our vision for social care for adults in England   204

Annex C: Glossary   **207**

Annex D: Abbreviations and acronyms   **225**

Introduction

This White Paper is an important new stage in building a world-class health and social care system. It meets the health challenges of the new century, and adapts to medical advances while responding to demographic changes in our society and increasing expectations of convenience and customer service from the public who fund the health service. These proposals, part of the Government's wider reform programme, will allow us to accelerate the move into a new era where the service is designed around the patient rather than the needs of the patient being forced to fit around the service already provided.

This White Paper builds on these principles and the significant progress, achieved through increased investment and reform, within the NHS over the last few years. There are 79,000 more nurses and 27,000 more doctors than in 1997 with more in training. Waiting lists and waiting times are dramatically down, helped in part by giving patients more choice and encouraging new providers within the NHS. The flexibility and freedoms offered to foundation hospitals have helped them improve care and service.

Deaths from cancer have fallen by 14 per cent, from heart disease by 31 per cent. Acute and emergency care in our hospitals has been transformed. Thousands of people in every community owe their lives to the extraordinary medical advances of recent decades and to the dedication of NHS staff.

The challenge for the NHS now is to maintain this progress while ensuring that GPs have the capacity to expand their services and respond to new demands from patients. To do this we will continue to refocus the system to meet these challenges. That is why GPs are being given greater control over their budgets and will be more accountable for the money they spend. This will allow them to acquire for their patients services from a broader range of providers within the NHS, voluntary and private sector. Crucially this is matched by greater choice for patients so they can take advantage of the new range of services on offer.

These reforms will also provide doctors, nurses and other staff with the ability and the incentives to tackle health problems earlier. It will lead to the greater emphasis on prevention and early intervention needed if we are to continue improving the nation's health. It will also meet the clear public preference for as much treatment at home or near home as possible. In both cases, it means a more efficient use of resources. This White Paper looks to see how we develop and expand these services.

It is also clear that we can make better use of the skills and experience of those working in the NHS to improve care, cut delays and make services more convenient. We want, for example, to expand the role of practice nurses and local pharmacists and encourage GPs to offer longer surgery hours.

While there has been real progress in the NHS, there is one area where improvement has not been fast enough. It is still the case that where you live has a huge impact on your well-being and the care you receive. These health inequalities remain much too stark – across social class and income groups, between different parts of the country and within communities. The new emphasis on prevention will help close the health gap; so will encouraging GPs and other providers to expand services in poorer communities.

These changes will be matched by much better links between health and social care. We will cut back the bureaucracy so local government and the NHS work effectively in tandem, and give customers a bigger voice over the care they receive.

All this will encourage local innovation, including the use of new providers, where necessary, to meet local needs. We want change to be driven, not centrally, but in each community by the people who use services and by the professionals who provide them.

Meeting these challenges will require a sustained shift in how we use the massive investment we are making as a country in health and care services.

None of this will be easy. Nor was slashing waiting lists, but the NHS has risen magnificently to this challenge. By giving frontline professionals and the public more say and control over the services they provide and receive, I am confident that we will continue building a high-quality health and social care system which meets the future needs and wishes of the country.

Tony Blair
Prime Minister

Foreword

This Government inherited health and social care services facing profound challenges. Years of under-investment, widening inequalities, soaring waiting lists, critical staff shortages, inflexible and unresponsive services – all needed tackling.

So we launched a major programme of investment and reform. Unprecedented investment in services, equipment, buildings and staff; demanding clinical standards; people's needs and wishes put at the heart of services, through choice and a greater drive to support people at home.

We focused first on improving hospitals and stabilising social care – and the results are there for all to see: more staff in more hospitals, providing better care for more people than ever before; our target for delivering home care was reached two years early; waiting lists tumbling, with waiting to be virtually abolished by 2008; care increasingly responsive to public needs and wants; the future of the NHS again seems secure.

But there is still more to do. These achievements bring us to a greater challenge still: of achieving health for all, not just improving health care. Our central question: how do we help every individual and every community get the most out of life in a country that has never been richer in opportunity than today?

And new challenges are emerging. A nation getting older – and sadly more obese. Fifteen million people with

long-term needs – such as diabetes, stroke, high blood pressure or cardiovascular conditions – needing better prevention and earlier care. The poorest areas too often with the poorest health and the poorest care. And people wanting a different approach to services, looking for real choices, more local care, taking greater control over their health, supported to remain independent wherever possible.

We will not meet these challenges by improving hospitals alone. Ninety per cent of people's contacts with the health service take place outside hospitals. Some 1.7 million people are supported by social care services at any given time. Increasingly, our primary, community and social care services will need to take the lead.

This White Paper builds upon the foundations we have laid in the last eight years, in particular our vision for public health set out in *Our Healthier Nation* and *Choosing Health*. It lays out a lasting and ambitious vision: by reforming and improving our community services, to create health and social care services that genuinely focus on prevention and promoting health and well-being; that deliver care in more local settings; that promote the health of all, not just a privileged few; and that deliver services that are flexible, integrated and responsive to peoples' needs and wishes.

And because we put people and patients first, we have held two unprecedented and innovative public consultations. Nearly 100,000 people were involved in the consultation on the adult social care Green Paper, *Independence, Well-being and Choice*. Over 40,000 people from all parts of the country participated enthusiastically in our deliberative consultation on this White Paper, culminating in a landmark, 1,000-person Citizens' Summit in Birmingham late last year.

I am very grateful to everyone who has contributed to the development of this White Paper. But I particularly want to thank our Citizens' Advisory Panel – the 10 people who worked with us throughout the public engagement process. As we listened to people and developed our own policy thinking, we went back to the panel to seek their views on our proposals. The next stage will be a further meeting with a larger group of participants in the summit and other 'Your Say' sessions, where my ministerial colleagues and I will present our White Paper and be held to account for the way in which we have responded to what the public have asked of us.

At the Citizens' Summit, I heard people clear in their desire for services to support them to stay healthy and give them more control of their lives; clear about their need for services that are convenient and closer to home; strong in their demand for greater access to GPs and other services; fair in their desire for good services to be available to all; and compassionate in their demand for services that give most help to those who need it most.

These concerns are at the heart of our proposals. And as a result of the

measures in this White Paper, we will see real change.

- People will be helped in their goal to remain healthy and independent.
- People will have real choices and greater access in both health and social care.
- Far more services will be delivered – safely and effectively – in the community or at home.
- Services will be integrated, built round the needs of individuals and not service providers, promoting independence and choice.
- Long-standing inequalities in access and care will be tackled.

Year on year, as health and social care budgets continue to rise, we will see more resources invested in prevention and community health and social care than in secondary care.

Previous governments have aspired to parts of this vision. But we are the first government to lay out both a comprehensive and compelling vision of preventative and empowering health and social care services and an effective programme for making this vision a reality. This White Paper truly represents the beginnings of a profound change: a commitment to real health and well-being for all.

Patricia Hewitt
Health Secretary

Executive summary

Reforming health and social care

1. Over the last few years, we have succeeded in improving many people's experience of health and social care. Hospital waiting lists and maximum waiting times are down. More people are supported in their home through intensive social care services. Cancer and cardiovascular services have changed dramatically, resulting in improved health outcomes for people with these conditions.

2. These improvements have been achieved through increased investment and by reform.

3. In the NHS, patients now have more choice of the hospital that they go to, with resources following their preferences. Patient choices have begun to play a role in developing the secondary care system, including driving down maximum waiting times. Because NHS Foundation Trusts have increased autonomy, they now use this to improve their performance. These reform principles – patient choice, resources following those choices and greater autonomy where it matters for local professionals – will now help to create the further improvements outlined in this White Paper.

4. We want people to have a real choice of the GP surgery to register with. The right of patients to choose one surgery over another will help to ensure that those surgeries are open at times that are suitable for them. Once registered, their GP needs to be empowered to commission the right services for their health care needs. This is why we are developing Practice Based Commissioning (PBC). If patient choice and PBC are in place, then health services will develop that are safe, high quality and closer to home, in the community. This has been a goal of health policy for some time and now it will be these reforms that directly provide the incentive for the health service to move services from secondary to primary care.

5. In social care, we have modernised services: setting national minimum standards; developing more choice of provider; investing in workforce training and regulation; supporting people to remain active and independent in their own homes; integrating social care services for children with other local authority services; and creating Directors of Children's Services to ensure a strong, co-ordinated focus. We have set out a future vision for adult services in our Green Paper *Independence, Well-being and Choice*.

6. This White Paper confirms the vision in the Green Paper of high-quality support meeting people's aspirations for independence and greater control over their lives, making services flexible and responsive to individual needs. We will build on what we have done, putting people more in control and shifting to a greater emphasis on prevention.

We will move towards fitting services round people not people round services.

The context of the White Paper

7. Britain today is a country of extraordinary opportunity. In an era of globalisation and rapid change, we are one of the world's most open economies and a technology leader. We have a world-class environment for e-commerce. Our biotech industry is second only to the US. There are more people in work than ever before after the longest unbroken record of economic growth since records began. We have never been better educated, better trained or better connected.

8. In the future, exponential advances in trade and technology hold the promise of a dramatically more productive economy and medical science offers us the prospect of living longer to enjoy it. Britain can face the future more ambitious than ever for a society in which each of us can fulfil our potential.

9. People are living longer. We need to ensure this means more years of health and well-being. Those aged over 65 with a long-term condition will double each decade. Healthy living starts early. Not being in work affects people's health. Feeling isolated or not supported affects people's health and well-being. And health inequalities are still much too stark – across socio-economic groups and in different

communities requiring targeted, innovative and culturally sensitive responses.

10. Medical science, assistive technology and pharmaceutical advances will continue to rapidly change the way in which people's lives can be improved by health and social care. It is important that the organisation of care fully reflects the speed of technological change. Procedures that could once only take place in hospital can now take place in the community. Assistive technology raises more possibilities and more people can be supported safely in their homes. Scientific advance will continue to challenge the way in which we organise our services. It would be wrong to allow a traditional method of delivery to hold back progress.

11. To keep pace with this ambition, our health and social care systems need to be able to improve to offer world-class services designed to fit with people's changing lives, their new expectations, ambitions and opportunities.

What the White Paper will achieve

12. This White Paper sets a new direction for the whole health and social care system. It confirms the vision set out in our Green Paper, *Independence, Well-being and Choice*. There will be a radical and sustained shift in the way in which services are delivered – ensuring that they are more personalised and that they fit into people's busy lives. We will give people a stronger voice so that they are the major drivers of service improvement.

The White Paper is aiming to achieve four main goals

13.   Health and social care services will provide **better prevention services with earlier intervention**. GP practices and Primary Care Trusts (PCTs) will work much more closely with local government services to ensure that there is early support for prevention.

14.   We will introduce a new NHS 'Life Check' for people to assess their lifestyle risks and to take the right steps to make healthier choices. This will be a personalised service in two parts. First, the assessment tool will be available either on-line as a part of Health Direct Online or downloaded locally in hard copy. Second, specific health and social care advice and support for those who need it will be available.

15.   We will bring in more support to maintain mental health and emotional well-being – something people raised with us as needing more attention. We will develop a high-profile campaign encouraging everyone to contribute to the drive for a Fitter Britain by 2012.

16.   People give a high priority to convenient access to social and primary care that they can choose and influence. We will give people **more choice and a louder voice**. We will give patients a guarantee of registration onto a GP practice list in their locality and simplify the system for doing this. To help them in making this choice, we will make it easier for people to get the information they need to choose a practice and understand what services are available in their area.

17.   To ensure that there are real choices for people, we will introduce incentives to GP practices to offer opening times and convenient appointments which respond to the needs of patients in their area. In social care, we will increase the take-up of direct payments by introducing new legislation to extend their availability to currently excluded groups and will pilot the introduction of individual budgets, bringing together several income streams from social care, community equipment, Access to Work, Independent Living Funds, Disability Facilities Grants and Supporting People. We will develop a risk management framework to enable people using services to take greater control over decisions about the way they want to live their lives.

18.   We need to **do more on tackling inequalities and improving access to community services**. We will ensure that local health and social care commissioners work together to understand and address local inequalities. There will also be a clear focus on those with ongoing needs. We will increase the quantity and quality of primary care in under-served, deprived areas. And we will ensure that people with particular needs get the services they require – young people, mothers, ethnic minorities, people with disabilities, people at the end of their lives, offenders and others. In social care, we will develop new ways to break down inequalities in access to services, for example through Social Care Link.

19.   There will be **more support for people with long-term needs**. People with long-term conditions will be supported to manage their conditions themselves with the right help from health and social care services. At the moment, half the people with long-term conditions are not aware of support or treatment options and do not have a clear plan that lays out what they can do for themselves to manage their condition better. If people have a clear understanding of their condition and what they can do, they are more likely to take control themselves.

20.   We will support people to do this by trebling the investment in the Expert Patient Programme, developing an 'information prescription' for people with long-term health and social care needs and for their carers, and developing assistive technologies to support people in their own homes.

21.   Many people with a long-term condition have social care as well as health care needs. To support a more integrated approach we will develop Personal Health and Social Care Plans and integrated social and health care records. To help people receive a more joined-up service, we will be establishing joint health and social care teams to support people with ongoing conditions who have the most complex needs. Carers are a vital part of the whole health and social care system – we will give them more support.

How are we going to achieve these improvements?

Practice Based Commissioning
22.   Practice Based Commissioning will give GPs more responsibility for local health budgets, while individual budget pilots will test how users can take control of their social care. These will act as a driver for more responsive and innovative models of joined-up support within communities, delivering better health outcomes and well-being, including a focus on prevention. It will be in the interests of primary care practices to develop more local services, which will provide better value for money.

23.   To assist this, we will explore changes to the Payment by Results (PBR) tariff to ensure it provides incentives to support the changes we want to see. PBC and changes to incentives together with pilots of

individual budgets will together revolutionise the way care is provided with a much stronger focus on personalised purchasing.

Shifting resources into prevention

24. We must set out a new direction for health and social care services to meet the future demographic challenges we face. We must reorientate our health and social care services to focus together on prevention and health promotion. This means a shift in the centre of gravity of spending. We want our hospitals to excel at the services only they can provide, while more services and support are brought closer to where people need it most.

More care undertaken outside hospitals and in the home

25. We aim to provide more care in more local, convenient settings, including the home. Over the next 12 months, we will work with the Royal Colleges to define clinically safe pathways within primary care for dermatology, ear, nose and throat medicine, general surgery, orthopaedics, urology and gynaecology. We will achieve this partly by introducing a new generation of community hospitals and facilities with strong ties to social care.

Better joining up of services at the local level

26. At the moment too much primary care is commissioned without integrating with the social care being commissioned by the local authority. There will be much more joint

commissioning between PCTs and local authorities. We will develop a procurement model and best practice guidance to underpin a joint commissioning framework for health and well-being.

27. To assist this, we will streamline budgets and planning cycles between PCTs and local authorities based on a shared, outcome-based performance framework. There will be aligned performance assessment and inspection regimes. Local Area Agreements should be a key mechanism for joint planning and delivery. There will be a strengthened role of Director of Adult Social Care, a wider role for Directors of Public Health, and more joint health and social care appointments. Work by a new National Reference Group for Health and Well-being will provide a sound evidence base for commissioning, including evidence from the Partnerships for Older People projects.

Encouraging innovation

28. Innovation will be encouraged by greater patient and user choice. The more that people can ensure that services are provided to suit their lives, the more there will be innovative approaches to service development. In primary care, we will assist this process by introducing new 'local triggers' on public satisfaction and service quality, to which PCTs will be expected to respond publicly. In social care, direct payments and individual budgets will ensure that services have to develop in a more responsive way.

**Allowing different providers
to compete for services**

29. In some deprived areas of the country there are fewer doctors per head of the population than in others. We will increase the quantity and quality of primary care in these areas through nationally supported procurement of new capacity with contracts awarded by local PCTs. To assist this process, we will remove barriers to entry for the 'third sector' as service providers for primary care.

Conclusions

30. This all adds up to an ambitious set of actions for change. They will not happen overnight. But, as our investment in health grows, primary care and community services will grow faster than secondary care. Future investment decisions will have to be taken with that shift in mind.

31. Our strategy is to put people more in control, to make services more responsive, to focus on those with complex needs and to shift care closer to home. We will also get better value for money. The same procedure in primary care can cost as little as one-third compared to secondary care. Wherever long-term conditions are well managed in the community, emergency bed days are diminished considerably.

32. People and patients want more safe health and social care in the community. That is not only better for people's health and well-being but provides better value for the public's money. This White Paper provides the framework to make that happen.

CHAPTER 1

Our ambition for community-based care

Our ambition for community-based care

This chapter on our strategic direction includes:

- what we heard people say in *Independence, Well-being and Choice* and in *Your health, your care, your say*;
- the challenges we face:
  - demographic change;
  - the need to radically realign systems;
  - the need to work with people to support healthier lifestyles;
- the new strategic direction:
  - more services in local communities closer to people's homes;
  - supporting independence and well-being;
  - supporting choice and giving people a say;
  - supporting people with high levels of need;
  - a sustained realignment of the health and social care system;
- support for the active, engaged citizen: making our vision a reality.

Our vision

1.1   People in the 21st century expect services to be fast, high quality, responsive and fitted around their lives. All public services should put the person who uses them at their heart. This applies especially to health and social care because all care is personal.

1.2   The care and support that we provide for people should enable them to make the most of their lives. The core values of the NHS and of social care already embody this principle.

1.3   In relation to social care, these values were clearly set out for adults in *Independence, Well-being and Choice*[1] as more choice, higher-quality services and greater control over their own lives. For the NHS, fair access to individual health care at the point of delivery, irrespective of ability to pay, has been its guiding theme since its foundation in 1948. But stating values is not enough.

1.4   This White Paper puts those values into practice in a modern world. For values to be relevant they must reflect our changing society; to be at all effective they have to be part of people's experience of care.

1.5   Our vision is of a new strategic direction for all the care and support services that people use in their communities and neighbourhoods. There are three simple themes, which came from people themselves.

- **Putting people more in control of their own health and care**
  People want to have more control of their own health, as well as their care. There is solid evidence that care is less effective if people feel they are not in control. A fundamental aim is to make the actions and choices of people who use services the drivers of improvement. They will be given more control over – and will take on greater responsibility for – their own health and well-being.
- **Enabling and supporting health, independence and well-being**
  We know the outcomes that people want for themselves: maintaining their own health, a sense of personal well-being and leading an independent life. *Choosing Health*[2] laid down the Government's broad programme for health improvement and this White Paper builds on that. Services in the community are at the frontline in delivering this programme.
- **Rapid and convenient access to high-quality, cost-effective care**
  When people access community services, they should do so in places and at times that fit in with the way they lead their lives. Organisational boundaries should not be barriers. Furthermore, services that would serve people better if they were placed in local communities should be located there and not in general hospitals. This will mean changes in the way in which local services are provided.

Listening to people

1.6 We set out to ensure that our proposals truly reflected the views of fellow citizens. Putting people more in control means first and foremost listening to them – putting them more in control of the policy setting process itself at national and then local level.

1.7 We therefore committed ourselves to two major consultation exercises designed to give people a genuine chance to influence national policy. The policies set out in this White Paper stem directly from what people have told us they want from health and social care in the future.

1.8 The consultation *Independence, Well-being and Choice* set out our aims for adult social care services. Around 100,000 people were involved. We published the results of that consultation in October 2005.[3] Our proposals received very strong support.

1.9 To understand more fully what people want from health and social care services working together, we commissioned a large, research-based consultation using an approach not tried before in England. The views of over 40,000 people were heard through questionnaires and face-to-face debate by people randomly selected from electoral registers and

Figure 1.1 Sources of participation in *Your health, your care, your say*

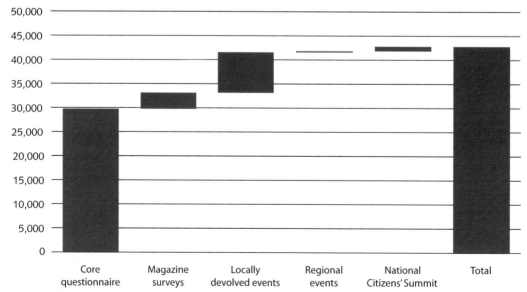

Source: Opinion Leader Research
Note: On-line survey totals include hard copy submissions as well as electronic
42,866 took part in total:
- 29,808 people filled in the core questionnaire (on-line and paper versions);
- 3,358 people filled in the magazine surveys in *Take a Break, Fit* and *Prime*;
- at least 8,460 people took part in local listening exercises;
- 254 people took part in the four regional deliberative events;
- 986 people took part in the national Citizens' Summit.

in local public meetings. The full report of this consultation – *Your health, your care, your say*[4] – is published at the same time as this White Paper.

1.10 In both consultations we paid particular attention to engaging with people who are heard less often. We worked with the voluntary sector to consult people from black and minority ethnic groups, older people and people with mental health problems, and developed text in 'easy-read' format and different languages. These proved popular – 28 per cent of all submissions received on *Independence, Well-being and Choice* used easy-read versions.

1.11 We established five policy task forces to reflect on what people were telling us in these consultations, and a wide range of stakeholders from all sectors also contributed.

1.12 The messages from these separate consultations were wholly consistent. People had a lot to say that was good about the services available now.

1.13 They praised the broad range of services free at the point of need. They praised a wide range of professionals for their expertise and care. They praised service innovations such as direct payments in social care, NHS Direct, NHS Walk-in Centres and one-stop shops, on-line booking of appointments and text message appointment reminders. They praised the shift towards earlier preventative services and greater personalisation of care.

1.14 However, the public were also clear that they want and expect to see improvements in primary and community services. Those who are satisfied say they think they may have been lucky and do not think the

Figure 1.2 The public's priorities

People said they want services that are based around their needs and that:
- help them to make choices and take control of their health and well-being by understanding their own health and lifestyle better, with more support on prevention and promoting their independence;
- offer easy access to help when they need it, in a way that fits their lives. To get the service they need, people want more information about where it is best for them to go;
- meet the whole of their needs, particularly if these are ongoing, and support their well-being and health, not just focusing on sickness or an immediate crisis; and
- are closer to where they live, provided these services are also safe and cost-effective.

Source: Opinion Leader Research

system consistently delivers a satisfactory service.

1.15 They believe that they should be able to rely on the quality of statutory services, but their experience does not always bear this out. Because they pay for them – either through taxation or local authority charges – people should have a say in how they are designed and delivered.

1.16 They were also realistic about resources. They acknowledged that finance is limited and that staff who do their best can be hard-pressed. But this did not mean that services could only get better if there was more money.

1.17 People were clear about what improvements they would like to see. These are summarised in Figure 1.2 – and a more complete description of what was said is given in Annex A.

Our challenge

1.18 What people think is important in itself – but even more so given what we know of changing needs over the next 10 to 15 years and beyond.

1.19 One of the greatest long-term challenges facing the health and social care system is to ensure that longer life means more years of health and well-being. Most illnesses are avoidable. The Government has a duty to help people maintain good health and to avoid disease and poor health. Unless we act, longer life could mean more years of ill-health and distress.

The burden of ongoing needs is set to increase significantly. Already almost a third of the population have such needs.

1.20 It has been estimated that the number of people over 65 years old with a long-term condition doubles each decade. The number of people over 85, the age group most likely to need residential or nursing home care, is expected to double by 2020.

1.21 Furthermore, 6 million people in this country care for family or friends. About 1.25 million of them provide care for over 50 hours each week. People who provide these long hours of care are twice as likely to be in poor health themselves, and need to be supported both in their own right and in their role as carers.

1.22 These estimates show not only that the burden of ill-health could significantly worsen but also that the pressure of demand on a tightly stretched NHS could increase severely. A system like today's NHS – which channels people into high-volume, high-cost hospitals – is poorly placed to cope effectively with this.

1.23 For people to receive responsive care and for resources to be more efficiently used, we need to realign the system radically away from its current pattern. Our collective challenge is to do all three of these:
- to meet the expectations of the public;

- to do so in a way that is affordable and gives value for money for the taxpayer; and
- to shift the system towards prevention and community-based care.

1.24 The challenge is also for each of us as individuals to take responsibility for our own lifestyles and aim for a healthy and fulfilling old age. We know that there are people who will find this more difficult than others, including those suffering from limiting long-term illness, disadvantaged groups such as homeless people and those living in areas of multiple deprivation. We will ensure that people who are disadvantaged are supported to meet this challenge and live healthy and fulfilling lives.

1.25 Some have argued that it is impossible for health and social care services to meet the collective challenge. Certainly, a health and social care system that fails to tackle the shortcomings identified by people during our consultations will not do so. There has to be a profound and lasting change of direction.

A new strategic direction

1.26 Our vision is to translate what people have said into a new strategic direction. A strategic shift that helps people to live more independently in their own homes and focus much more on their own well-being. A strategic shift aimed at supporting choice and giving people more say over decisions that affect their daily lives. The more people have the right to choose, the more their preferences will improve services.

1.27 This will not, however, be at the expense of those with high levels of need for whom high-quality services – and, where necessary, protection for those unable to safeguard themselves – must be in place. In delivering this strategic shift, we are committed to a health and social care system that promotes fairness, inclusion and respect for people from all sections of society, regardless of their age, disability, gender, sexual orientation, race, culture or religion, and in which discrimination will not be tolerated.

1.28 Our longer-term aim is to bring about a sustained realignment of the whole health and social care system. Far more services will be delivered – safely and effectively – in settings closer to home; people will have real choices in both primary care and social care; and services will be integrated and built round the needs of individuals and not service providers. Year on year, as NHS budgets rise, we will see higher growth in prevention, primary and community care than in secondary care, and also resources will shift from the latter to the former.

1.29 It is important to be clear from the outset that we see a new direction for the 'whole system'. This refers to all health and social care services provided in community settings. Specifically, these are:

- **social care:** the wide range of services designed to support people to maintain their independence, enable them to play a fuller part in society, protect them in vulnerable situations and manage complex relationships;
- **primary care:** all general practice, optician and pharmacy-based services available within the NHS (this White Paper does not include dentistry);
- **community services:** the full range of services provided outside hospitals by nurses and other health professionals (for example physiotherapists, chiropodists and others);
- other settings including transport and housing that contribute to community well-being.

Making our vision a reality

1.30 The purpose of this White Paper is not merely to provide a vision of what needs to be done, but to provide the means for achievement. Governments in the past have promoted elements of this vision. But this is the first time that a government has both laid out a compelling vision of preventative and empowering health and social care services and has put in place the levers for making this change happen.

1.31 *Independence, Well-being and Choice* set out a clear vision for adult social care which was overwhelmingly supported in the consultation (see Annex B). This White Paper confirms that vision and puts in place practical steps to turn it into a reality.

1.32 A powerful force for change in the NHS will be the reform framework, described recently in *Health reform in England: Update and next steps*.[5] There, we laid out how greater patient choice and control, a wider range of providers with greater freedoms, stronger commissioning, new payment mechanisms and better information and inspection will all underpin the changes we are making.

1.33 For the NHS, between now and 2008 there will be a major continued focus on improving access to hospital care through the 18-week maximum wait target. With the quality of secondary care assured in this way, this White Paper moves on to the opportunities opened up by Practice Based Commissioning (PBC) and the new tariff (Payment by Results).

1.34 GPs and community-based professionals are closest to individual users and patients and, together with them, make the key decisions. So under PBC, GPs and primary care professionals – working closely with Primary Care Trusts (PCTs) – will have greater capability than ever before. They will have greater freedoms than ever before to commission health and social care services for the individual person.

1.35 In the past – and even under GP fund holding – primary care professionals controlled just a fraction of health resources. Under PBC, primary care practices will control the bulk of local health resources and will be able to use them to bring decisions closer to people.

1.36 The impact of choice and stronger commissioning will be greatly enhanced by the Payment by Results (PBR) reform. This sets a tariff that all providers receive for NHS work. The tariff provides powerful incentives for change.

1.37 It makes real to commissioners the benefits of promoting health or improving care for people with long-term needs, by making clear the costs of preventable illnesses, avoidable emergency admissions, poor medication prescription and use or lack of preventative investment in social care.

1.38 Given that the tariff is fixed, it also encourages commissioners to seek out providers who offer better quality care, or develop local alternatives that deliver, safely and effectively, the services that people want to use. It was first introduced in the context of the reform of the hospital sector. For this reason, not everything about the current structure of the tariff aligns with the radical shift that this White Paper seeks to achieve. So we will improve it.

Well-being in our communities

1.39 Social care and primary health care services are embedded in our communities. They are part of the pattern of our daily lives. We will shift the whole system towards the active, engaged citizen in his or her local community and away from monolithic, top-down paternalism.

1.40 We see the foundation of this beginning at pre-birth, through infancy and childhood, and extending throughout people's lives into old age. Making sure that from the beginning we give our children the right start in life is particularly important to achievements.

1.41 For the first time, patients and primary care professionals will be in the driving seat of reform, using local resources to invest in services and shape care pathways which are most appropriate for local people. As a result, the vision and reforms laid out in this White Paper will ensure that we achieve the best possible outcomes for the whole of the NHS budget by reshaping the way the whole system works.

1.42 We will also redesign the system 'rules' so they push decisions closer to the communities affected by them. The framework of priorities for the NHS and social care – set out in *National Standards, Local Action*[6] and in the new Public Service Agreements – emphasises four main areas: public health, long-term conditions, access and patient experience.

1.43 We will be taking work forward to relate these closely to the seven outcomes of adult social care (see paragraph 2.63). We will aim to produce a single set of outcomes across both social and health care which are consistent with those being consulted on in 2006 for use across all of local government.

1.44 There will be a new partnership between local authorities and reformed PCTs. They are both 'commissioners'. This is the term we use to refer to the full set of activities they undertake to make sure that services funded by them, on behalf of the public, are used to meet the needs of the individual fairly, efficiently and effectively.

1.45 Commissioning has to be centred on the person using the service. Local authorities and PCTs together will focus on community well-being, with much more extensive involvement of people who use services and surveys of their views. They will take action when services do not deliver what local people need or if there are inequalities in quantity or quality of care. Together, they will drive the radical realignment of the whole local system, which includes services like transport, housing and leisure.

1.46 We need innovative providers – whether state-owned, not-for-profit or independent businesses, like primary care practices, pharmacies and many social care providers – that work together as part of a joined-up system. We also need to support different

approaches from non-traditional providers. We will encourage the independent and voluntary sectors to bring their capabilities much more into play in developing services that respond to need.

1.47 We need strategies for workforce development that support radical shifts in service delivery and equip staff with the skills and confidence to deliver excellent services, often in new settings. Staff will increasingly need to bridge hospital and community settings in their work. And we will work with staff organisations to make sure the changes are implemented in a way that is consistent with good employment practice.

1.48 We need robust systems of independent regulation that guarantee safety and deliver assured quality while identifying areas for improvement.

1.49 Importantly, we need to ensure that there is a strong voice for people using services and for local communities in the way in which the whole health and care system is designed and works. This may well involve looking afresh at where services are best provided locally and making changes, after full consultation, to the balance between hospital and community settings.

Resources

1.50 The funding arrangements for the NHS and local authorities are different, reflecting their different roles as set out in Chapter 4. The majority of this White Paper's proposals for local authorities are about better partnership working with stakeholders to deliver more effective services, while also achieving better value for money from existing resources. However, where there are additional costs for some elements of the proposals, we will make specific resources available to fund them, without placing unfunded new burdens upon local authorities or putting any pressure on council tax.

1.51 We will consider with key stakeholders, including local government, the costs as policies are developed further. We will review the financial impact on local authorities after the changes have been implemented, to ensure that the correct level of funding has been provided and to test the assumptions made.

Our proposals

1.52 We set out in this White Paper how we will do all of this. The next chapters explain our proposals for:
- helping people to lead healthier and more independent lives (Chapter 2);
- more responsive and accessible care (Chapters 3 and 4);
- better support for people with ongoing needs (Chapter 5);
- a wider range of services in the community (Chapter 6);
- ensuring these reforms put people in control (Chapter 7);
- the underpinning changes required to implement these ideas (Chapter 8);
- the actions and timetable for implementation (Chapter 9).

References

1   *Independence, Well-being and Choice: Our vision for the future of social care for adults in England* (Cm 6499), The Stationery Office, March 2005

2   *Choosing Health: Making healthier choices easier* (Cm 6374), The Stationery Office, November 2004

3   *Responses to the consultation on adult social care in England: Analysis of the feedback from the Green Paper*, Department of Health, October 2005

4   *Your health, your care, your say: Research report*, Opinion Leader Research, January 2006, www.dh.gov.uk

5   *Health reform in England: Update and next steps,* Department of Health, December 2005

6   *National Standards, Local Action: Health and social care standards* and *Planning Framework 2005/06–2007/08*, Department of Health, July 2004

CHAPTER 2

Enabling health, independence and well-being

Enabling health, independence and well-being

This chapter on health, independence and well-being includes the following commitments:

- developing an NHS 'Life Check' starting in Primary Care Trust (PCT) spearhead areas;

- better support for mental health and emotional well-being: promoting good practice; demonstration sites for people of working age, as part of our action to help people with health conditions and disabilities to remain in, or return to, work; access to computerised cognitive behaviour therapy;

- local leadership of well-being: improving commissioning and joint working through defining and strengthening the roles of Directors of Public Health (DPHs) and Directors of Adult Social Services (DASSs);

- better partnership working in local areas: a new outcomes framework; aligning performance measures, assessments and inspection; aligning planning and budget cycles for the NHS and local authorities;

- stronger local commissioning: shifting towards prevention and early support; expanding the evidence base through Partnerships for Older People Projects (POPPs); National Reference Group for Health and Well-Being; re-focusing the Quality and Outcomes Framework (QOF);

- national leadership: stronger leadership for social care within the Department of Health; a new Fitter Britain campaign.

Introduction

2.1 People want to stay as healthy, active and independent as possible. We each have a responsibility for our own health and well-being throughout our lives.

2.2 At the same time, the Government – as well as the citizen – has a role in promoting healthier, longer lives lived to the full. In our society, not everyone has the same opportunities or capacity to take action to improve their own health and well-being. We will build on and strengthen the opportunities for improving the health of the population set out in *Choosing Health*. Public bodies can and should do more to support individuals and give everyone an equal chance to become and stay healthy, active and independent.

2.3 People in the *Your health, your care, your say* consultation reflected this view strongly. They said that they wanted to take responsibility for their health and to be helped to do that. This echoed the strong messages in *Independence, Well-being and Choice* where people wanted services to support their independence, put them in control and focus on the prevention of ill-health and promote well-being at all stages of their lives.

2.4 These are not idle aspirations. As a nation, we are faced with the real possibility that – due to lifestyle changes – **our children will not live as long as their parents unless there is a shift towards healthier living.**[1] Millions of working days are lost each year through ill-health, with mental health problems and stress now the most frequent causes of this.[2] Services also must respond to the needs of the ageing population, supporting people to continue to live full, healthy and independent lives as they grow older.

2.5 People also felt strongly that those at greatest disadvantage need more help than others. The two Wanless reports[3] highlighted the need for citizens to be fully engaged with their health and for their health service to deliver better health outcomes for the poorest in our communities and to ease pressures and costs for the NHS in the long-run. *Choosing Health* outlined a cross-government strategy for delivering this, in partnership with local services, and *Independence, Well-being and Choice* set out proposals for promoting social inclusion for all those needing support to maintain their independence.

2.6 Preventing ill-health and enabling people to play a full role in their local communities are also key parts of the Government's work on regeneration and building sustainable communities. And the quality of the environment, for example of our air and water, is vital to health and an important aspect of health protection. Access to green spaces, clean and safe open air spaces where people can meet and exercise informally, and planning and design that encourage walking and cycling are all important factors in supporting health and well-being.

Childhood

2.7 Healthy living starts before we are born. The evidence is unmistakable. Health later in life is influenced by such factors as whether mothers smoke or breastfeed their babies. The children of overweight parents are more likely to grow up overweight. What food and drinks we see as desirable and healthy are determined at an early age. Early relationships may affect later resilience and mental well-being. Healthy living must therefore start at the earliest opportunity and should continue as part of schooling.

2.8 *Every Child Matters*[4] set out our aspirations to maximise the health and well-being and achievement of all children. We are working to achieve this through a major reform programme which includes the integration of local services in children's trusts, the implementation of the *National Service Framework for Children, Young People and Maternity Services*[5] and better support for parents and carers.

2.9 Because health and development in early childhood are crucial influences on health and other outcomes throughout life, we have made a major investment in transforming the life chances of the most disadvantaged children aged under five through the Sure Start local programmes. The intention is for parents, from the time they know they are expecting a baby, to be supported by integrated health, childcare, early education and family support services that target those most at risk of poor outcomes.

2.10 In the current Childcare Bill, the Government is proposing a new duty on local authorities, working with their partners, to improve the outcomes of all young children under school age and to reduce inequalities in these outcomes. The main delivery vehicle for the strategy will be the development of Sure Start Children's Centres in every community, bringing together health, family and parenting support, childcare and other services. There are currently about 400 Children's Centres and the number is set to rise to 1,000 by September 2006, 2,500 by 2008 and to 3,500 by 2010.

2.11 Following *Choosing Health*, we are also improving support for school-age children. All schools should promote the physical health and emotional well-being of children and young people, including through access to nutritious, well-balanced food, personal, social and health education, and to opportunities for

Peer mentoring in Warrington

Starting at a new school can be daunting. In Warrington, one school has hit on the solution of pairing older pupils with new entrants.

Year 8 pupils at William Beaumont School have been discussing issues such as the secondary school culture, healthy eating, bullying and sport with Year 6 pupils at local primary schools. The Year 8 mentors are given training in advance. They then work on a one-to-one basis with primary school pupils who may struggle to cope with the move from a small primary school to a much larger secondary school.

Everyone has benefitted from the scheme. The mentors say they have become more confident, felt responsible and are enjoying their own lessons more, while the mentees say they are less anxious and happier about their impending move.

Thirteen-year-old Beth Caddick was mentored when she was in Year 6 and is now a mentor herself: "It's great being able to help others and it makes you feel good about yourself. You can answer all their questions and problems. It was years ago when the teachers were at school, wasn't it, so we probably have more of an idea what it's like." Her mother, Maxine, is really pleased with how the programme has helped her gain confidence. "It's enabled her to participate in other activities that she wouldn't have had the confidence to do in the past. It makes her feel a better person and she's achieved a lot. She has come out of herself and I'm really proud of her."

Teachers have seen the benefits, with one primary school teacher remarking that: "Self-esteem has improved and children are much more prepared for the move." The William Beaumont school has seen a dramatic decline in the number of Year 7 pupils having difficulty with the change of schools.

physical activity and sport. We are working with schools, through our Healthy Schools programme and other initiatives, to achieve this, and we are investing £840 million over five years in order to expand the range of services – including healthy living advice and support services – on offer to children and local communities through extended schools.

2.12 We know that the transition between primary and secondary education can be particularly testing for some young people.[6] Difficulties encountered at this pivotal stage can have profound consequences for future social and educational progress, so support at this life stage is crucial. The peer mentoring pilot projects in 180 secondary schools announced in *Support for parents: the best start for children*[7] will provide additional support for vulnerable young people throughout secondary education.

2.13 The *Youth Matters* Green Paper[8] recognised the inseparable link between good emotional and physical health and success in learning and achievement. Support for both emotional and physical health is a core part of the Green Paper's proposals to promote more integrated, multi-disciplinary support for young people. Thirteen pilots for these new integrated forms of support are now under way. Life skills and emotional resilience acquired in childhood and adolescence help people cope with challenges throughout their lives. *Youth Matters* set out a range of proposals for making health services more responsive to young people's needs, and the Government will shortly publish its response to the consultation and next steps.

2.14 Improving the way key individuals and organisations safeguard and promote the welfare of children is crucial to improving outcomes for children. Section 11 of the Children Act 2004 places a duty on key people and bodies, including Strategic Health Authorities (SHAs), PCTs, NHS Trusts and Foundation Trusts, to make arrangements to ensure that their functions are carried out with regard to the need to safeguard and promote the welfare of children and young people. Effective information sharing by professionals is central to safeguarding and promoting the welfare of children. The Government is expected to publish further guidance on this during 2006.

People of working age

2.15 Health and well-being also matter in adult life. In particular, work is an important part of people's adult lives. There is good evidence that someone who is out of work is more likely to be in poor health and use services more frequently. People who are out of work for longer periods are at greater risk of losing their sense of well-being and confidence, which may lead to longer-term mental health problems and long-term detachment from the labour market. There is a strong link between unemployment, social exclusion and health inequalities in this country.

2.16 Health conditions and disabilities, if not appropriately managed and supported, can lead to job loss and long-term benefit dependency, with all the associated consequences not just for individuals but for their families. Equally, good health and emotional well-being can assist people to enter work and maintain fitness for work.

2.17 The Department of Health is working with the Department for Work and Pensions and the Health and Safety Executive to address these issues through *Health, work and well-being – caring for our future*.[9] This strategy seeks to break the link between ill-health and inactivity, to advance the prevention of ill-health and injury, and to encourage good management of occupational health issues. It also aims to transform opportunities for people to recover from illness, while at work, maintaining their independence and sense of worth. By ensuring equal rights and opportunity for all, not only will individuals benefit, but employers and the economy as a whole will gain from the huge potential that people have to offer.

2.18 The Government's planned welfare reforms will take the health, work and well-being agenda forwards. We have already seen great success from local partnership working, led by PCTs, in the Pathways to Work pilots. Over 19,500 people with a health condition or disability have been helped by the pilots to make a return to work.

2.19 As the first point of contact for people with health conditions, GPs and primary care teams play a key role in providing the support to patients that allows them to remain in work or to return to work quickly. The Department for Work and Pensions is developing a range of initiatives to provide the support necessary for GPs to offer this help to their patients. Initiatives include training in fitness for work issues, piloting access to employment advice and support, and

CASE STUDY

Improving mental health in London

Pioneering work in mental health is going on across the capital. In South London the NHS is working with local voluntary and community services to help people back to work as part of the New Deal for Disabled People. South West London and St George's Mental Health Trust runs an exemplary employment service which uses employment advisers to place referred clients. In 2004/05 it managed to place 922 clients in jobs and 90 per cent remained in employment.

North East London and the East London and The City Mental Health Trusts are also developing an NHS Live project which focuses on employment for people with a mental illness. Rita Dove, a mental health user development co-ordinator in East London, says: "We get a range of issues that I have to help with. Often it's a question of just trying to build up someone's confidence and at other times someone might not be aware of what they are entitled to beyond their direct mental health problems. People who come here are very vulnerable but I try to encourage them to have responsibility for themselves, even in the smallest way. One person now does the washing up here and gets paid £5 and that has started to help them build their confidence."

They [leisure centres] do have facilities for the wheelchair user, but most of the time the lift is broken and they sometimes say they can't get it repaired. Obviously if the lift doesn't work you can't go for a swim there.

RESPONDENT TO *INDEPENDENCE, WELL-BEING AND CHOICE*

piloting an occupational health helpline for GPs. The proposals contained in this White Paper will further enhance this process.

Older people

2.20 Our aims for promoting health and well-being in old age are:

- to promote higher levels of physical activity in the older population;
- to reduce barriers to increased levels of physical activity, mental well-being and social engagement among excluded groups of older people;
- to continue to increase uptake of evidence-based disease prevention programmes among older people.

2.21 *Choosing Health*, the *National Service Framework for Older People* and the Green Paper, *Independence, Well-being and Choice* set out our vision for promoting health, independence and well-being for older people, as well as describing some of the levers for effecting change.

2.22 A cross-government group will drive the broad health and well-being agenda forwards with involvement of key stakeholders from the National Coalition for Active Ageing. Detailed plans will be set out in the forthcoming National Clinical Director for Older People's report *Next Steps for Older People's National Service Framework*.

2.23 This work fits within wider cross-government policy for older people, described in *Opportunity Age*.[10] It links to our recently published report on older people and social exclusion, *A Sure Start to Later Life: Ending Inequalities for Older People*,[11] which announced the £10 million programme Link-Age Plus. This will include a network of one-stop centres developed and controlled locally and containing services such as health, social care, housing, leisure, education, volunteering and social opportunities.

Disabled people and people with high support needs

2.24 These strategies complement the 20-year strategy *Improving the life chances of disabled people*,[12] which focuses on independent living, choice and control for all disabled adults.

2.25 The Supporting People programme, launched in April 2003, enables the provision of housing-related support services that help people with a wide range of needs to live independently and to avoid unnecessary or premature hospitalisation or use of institutional care. The programme covers a broad

30   Our health, our care, our say: a new direction for community services

range of vulnerable groups, including people with disabilities and older people. Through *Creating Sustainable Communities: Supporting Independence*,[13] the Government is consulting on how best to build on and take forward the programme, including through improving co-ordination and integration of care and support services for those who receive both.

2.26 This chapter now sets out what more the Government will do to support people to look after their own health and well-being: joining up local services better, shifting the system towards prevention and providing effective national leadership

Helping people to look after their own health and well-being

2.27 People want to keep themselves well, and take control of their own health. This came through clearly in our consultation. People asked for more help to do this, through better

information, advice and support. In particular, people strongly supported the idea of regular check-ups as a way of helping them to look after themselves, and reduce demand on conventional health and care services. Avoidable illness matters to individuals and their families but it also matters to society and the economy. We all bear the costs of days lost at work and expenditure on avoidable care. Regular check-ups was voted the top 'people's priority' at the national Citizens' Summit.

2.28 There is, however, clear evidence that simply offering routine physical checks, such as cholesterol testing, to everyone in the population is not an effective way of identifying people at risk of disease and ill-health.[14] Nor would it be a good use of the considerable resources which would have to go into developing such a global screening programme.

NHS 'Life Check'
2.29 The best way of empowering people to take charge of their own health and well-being is to focus on the major risk factors that may affect their health:
* Higher obesity rates are predicted to lead to a rise in strokes, heart attacks and Type 2 diabetes. Only 37 per cent of men and 25 per cent of women are achieving recommended physical activity targets.[15] Rates of obesity are rising steadily.

Figure 2.1 People's top priorities at the Citizens' Summit in Birmingham

Which of these are your top priorities?

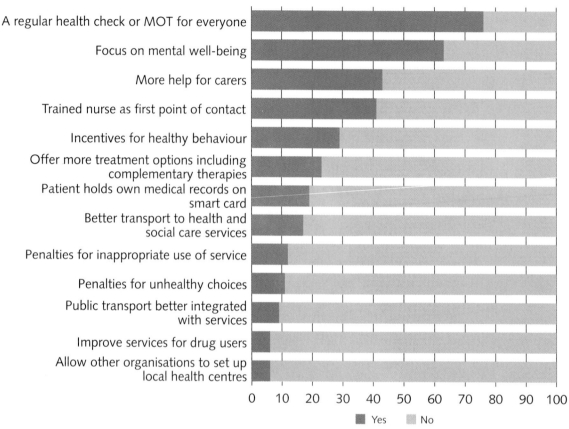

Source: Citizens' Summit, Birmingham, 2005
N = ~986

- Smoking is the single greatest cause of illness and premature death in England today, killing an estimated 86,500 people a year, accounting for a third of all cancers and a seventh of cardiovascular disease. A significant proportion of the population still smokes. Smoking disproportionately affects the least well-off. Some 31 per cent of manual groups smoke, compared with 20 per cent in non-manual groups.

- Between 15,000 and 22,000 deaths and 150,000 hospital admissions each year are associated with alcohol misuse. A significant proportion of the population drinks more than the maximum recommended weekly amounts (14 units for women and 21 units for men) and many young people are taking increased risks by binge drinking.

Figure 2.2 Predicted growth in obesity-related disease by 2030

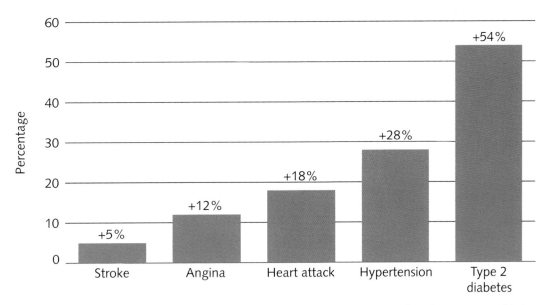

Source: Living in Britain 2004: Results from the 2002 General Household Survey; National Food Survey 2000 Table B1

Figure 2.3 Obesity rates in England

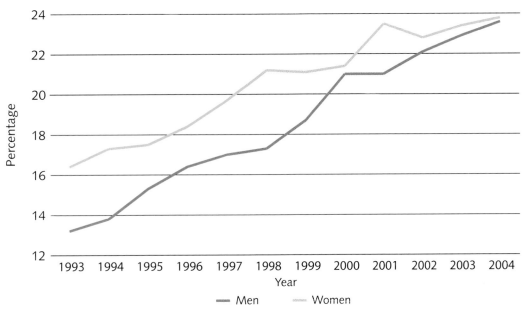

Source: Health Survey for England 2004

Figure 2.4 Smoking rates in England

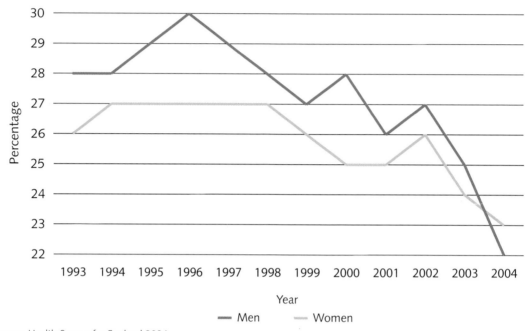

Year

— Men — Women

Source: Health Survey for England 2004

Figure 2.5 Population drinking more than maximum recommended weekly amount

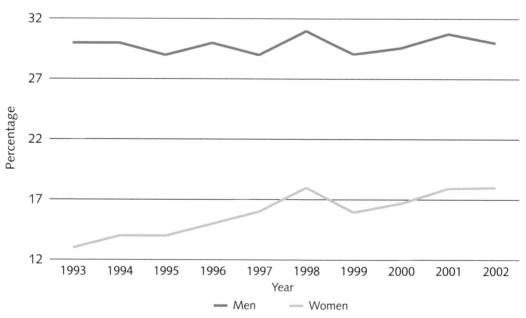

Year

— Men — Women

Source: Health Survey for England 2004

- Mental illness and stress-related conditions are now the most common cause of sickness absence and are a common cause of social exclusion among older people. One in four consultations with a GP concern mental health problems.
- Sexually transmitted infections continue to rise. Up to one in ten young people aged under 25 may be infected with chlamydia, leading to pelvic inflammatory disease, ectopic pregnancy and infertility.

2.30 We will therefore develop a new NHS 'Life Check' service to help people – particularly at critical points in their lives – to assess their own risk of ill-health. The NHS 'Life Check' will be based on a range of risk factors, such as those outlined above, and on awareness of family history. The service will be developed and evaluated in 2007, with a view to wider roll-out thereafter.

2.31 The NHS 'Life Check' will be a personalised service in two parts:
- an initial assessment for people to complete themselves;
- offers of specific advice and support on the action people can take to maintain and improve health and, if necessary, referral for more specialist diagnoses for those who need it.

2.32 The NHS 'Life Check' will be available on-line as part of Health Direct Online, or locally on paper.

Where people complete the self-assessment on-line, they will be able to store it in their own personal HealthSpace,[16] as part of a life-long personal health plan. They will have the option to share their assessment electronically with their general practice surgery. It can then be held as part of their electronic care record to help inform health professionals about the lifestyle risks and family history factors that may affect their long-term health and well-being.

2.33 People whose initial self-assessment indicates that they are at significant risk of poor health will be able to discuss the outcome with a health trainer. The discussion will include looking at what action they can take to improve their own health, for example through diet or exercise. It will also cover the further help they might want to seek from local services, including, where appropriate, referral to seek medical advice and follow-up from more specialist services and the development of a personal health plan. Follow-up action may involve a range of health and social care services. For example, for young children this may involve services provided at Children's Centres, including parental advice; and for adults in work, support may be provided in the workplace through occupational health services.

2.34 We will develop the approach to take account of the changing needs of people in their early years, childhood, early adulthood, working and later years. The Department of Health will start by working jointly with the Department for Education and Skills to test the approach for children at key ages, including within the first year and at the transition from primary to secondary education. Self-assessment by parents will be included as an integral part of considering the health of their children. For the youngest children we will look at how the 'Life Check' is part of the child health promotion programme, linking it to the routine developmental assessments and other support currently provided to parents to ensure a joined-up approach. For adults we will initially develop the approach for people around the age of 50, then move on to test at other key ages. We will help parents, children and other key carers understand and engage in behaviour changes to reduce the risks of binge drinking, smoking, poor sexual health, poor diet, and low levels of physical exercise, all of which can have negative effects on future adult health.

2.35 The NHS 'Life Check' will be developed in areas with the worst health and deprivation (the spearhead areas), in consultation with groups of people who are least likely to access advice provided through conventional services. It will be led by health trainers who are already being recruited in those spearhead areas.

2.36 Development work will include looking at how NHS 'Life Check' should link into wider local strategies, particularly action on neighbourhood renewal and tackling inequalities.

In 2007/08, as the technology to deliver rolls out, the NHS 'Life Check' will become more widely available in formats and languages to meet everyone's needs. The approach will be tested to ensure that it works for the many different groups in our society, particularly those at greatest disadvantage and those who may need assistance in completing the self-assessment, and it will take account of the needs of carers.

Mental health and emotional well-being

2.37 Emotional well-being and resilience are fundamental to people's capacity to get the most out of life, for themselves and for their families. In the consultation people made it clear that they wanted action to help them maintain mental and emotional well-being just as much as physical health and fitness. There is much that can be done to reduce the frequency of the more common illnesses such as anxiety and depression, and the widespread misery that does not reach the threshold for clinical diagnosis but nevertheless reduces the quality of life of thousands of people. Helping people in these situations will help them to lead happier, more fulfilled and productive lives.

2.38 Straightforward positive steps that everyone can take were set out in *Making it possible*[17] – a good practice guide to improving people's mental health and well-being. They include:
- keeping physically active;
- eating well;

I think that being mentally healthy is more than just having medical treatment, it's about quality of life.

RESPONDENT TO *INDEPENDENCE, WELL-BEING AND CHOICE*

CASE STUDY

Keeping Healthy in Hull

In Hull, the Looking Good, Feeling Good programme is helping people understand how to live healthy lives. The scheme is the brainchild of Christine Ebeltoft, community health development worker, and Tracy Taylor and June Carroll, two local practice nurses.

The programme has been run in five different locations throughout Eastern Hull in church halls, community centres and the local Women's Centre. This enables health workers to reach out to people who might not use traditional health services, and it is helping people stay well.

The content of the ten-week programme to encourage lifestyle change was developed with the people who would use it. They wanted a programme that offered exercise, weight management and looked at various other issues such as smoking, food labelling, stress and nutrition.

Christine said: "It's very much about prevention rather than cure. We are not here to dictate to people about their lifestyle, just to give them information on other options and advice. It's not about putting people on a diet. It's all about lifestyle change."

- if you do drink, drink in moderation;
- valuing yourself and others;
- talking about your feelings;
- keeping in touch with friends and loved ones;
- caring for others;
- getting involved and making a contribution;
- learning new skills;
- doing something creative;
- taking a break;
- asking for help.

2.39 We will take steps to make these simple messages more widely known by ensuring that mental well-being is included in the social marketing strategy currently being developed to support *Choosing Health*.

Westbury Fields for ever

Mildred and Norman Jenkins were the first residents to move in to Westbury Fields Retirement Home, a residential village for older people in Bristol, run by the charity St Monica Trust. Both are in their seventies.

"My husband's been a paraplegic for almost 18 years, I'd had a couple of bouts of cancer and we were getting older, so when we read about Westbury Fields in the local paper we thought it would be a good move for us. It's a question of security. If there are any problems we can press the emergency button and someone will come to help us and my husband has care and support. It means we've been able to keep our independence, but it has also taken a lot of pressure off both of us, and our daughters. They know that if there is an emergency there's someone on hand.

"The surroundings here are very nice, and there's plenty to do. I go to art classes, there are poetry readings, a library and clubs, and a minibus for outings or shopping. We have the companionship of people our own age and we can join in with activities or not, it's up to us. We're very happy we decided to come here."

Westbury Fields is home to more than 200 older people who occupy 150 retirement/sheltered apartments and a 60-bed care home. The aim of the village is to encourage a lively, balanced community ranging from active independent residents to those requiring a high degree of support.

2.40 As well as helping people to increase their own positive mental health and resilience, we also need to address external factors such as violence and abuse or workplace stress which may pose a risk to their well-being. Each local area needs to have a mental health promotion strategy which addresses these issues as well as the issues of individual lifestyles.

2.41 *Making it possible* identified the criteria that could be used to identify good practice in local mental health promotion strategies. Good practice demonstrated:
* local needs assessment;
* cross-sector ownership, governance and resourcing;

- links to wider initiatives to improve health and social care outcomes;
- clear statement of what success would look like and how it should be measured;
- evidence-based interventions;
- building public mental health/mental health promotion capacity;
- developing public mental health intelligence.

2.42 Sometimes, however, people are reluctant to accept that they have mental health needs, and may be unwilling to talk about feelings or ask for help due to fear and lack of understanding. **We will strengthen our efforts to improve public understanding of mental health issues, building on the existing Shift campaign to counteract stigma and discrimination.**

2.43 We do not yet know how to prevent the most severe forms of mental illness such as schizophrenia and bipolar disorder. However, we do know that early intervention can reduce the length of episodes of ill-health and prevent some of the longer-term health and social consequences of severe mental illness.

2.44 Universal services, such as transport, housing and leisure services, including access to sports, arts and culture, can play a crucial role in facilitating social contacts and supporting social inclusion. Older people living alone are particularly vulnerable to isolation and loneliness. A number of pilots are currently testing approaches to support for older people, including promoting good mental health. The recently published Social Exclusion Unit's report *A Sure Start to Later Life* on excluded older people also sets out proposals for support for this group.

2.45 For people who are clearly exhibiting signs of mild depression or anxiety, psychological ('talking') therapies offer a real alternative to medication. They can extend choice, reduce waiting times for treatment and help to keep people in work or support them to return to work.

2.46 As part of the Government's commitment to expand access to psychological therapies, we plan to establish two demonstration sites. These demonstration sites will focus on people of working age with mild to moderate mental health problems, with the aim of helping them to remain in or return to work. They will aim to establish an evidence base for the effectiveness of such therapies and to support the extension to non-working age people and those with moderate to severe mental illness.

2.47 New technology is also increasing the treatment options available in mental health. Computerised cognitive behaviour therapy (CCBT) allows people to take charge of their own treatment. The National Institute for Health and Clinical Excellence (NICE) will publish a full appraisal of five specific packages for the delivery of CCBT in February 2006. **Where this guidance, on the basis of clinical and cost effectiveness, recommends the use of a particular package in surgeries, clinics and other settings, such as community centres and schools, the Department of Health will consider how PCTs can best be supported in accessing the packages.**

2.48 In the past, GPs have sought to respond appropriately to the needs of people with complex social, physical and psychological care needs. This role has been extremely challenging because these groups' needs often cannot be managed confidently by GPs within existing primary care services, nor can they be appropriately referred to secondary care, which tends to be focused on those with severe and enduring mental illness.

2.49 Primary care offers significant opportunities to tackle ill-health, including:
- provision of psychological therapies for mild to moderate mental health problems;
- introduction of the 'stepped care model' of service provision recommended by NICE;
- development of new mental health worker roles in primary care, such as graduate primary workers;
- development of GPs with Special Interests (GPwSIs);

- opportunities to use the QOF to improve the care provided to people with mental health problems.

2.50 People with common mental health problems will be given more control over their lives by providing them with access to evidence-based psychological interventions, including cognitive behaviour therapy (CBT), CCBT, and other talking therapies. These services will be provided in non-stigmatising primary and community locations and will be complemented by access to employment advisers, who will work with people with common mental health problems to help them to stay in or return to work.

2.51 We need to ensure that all these services are of a high quality. However, there are currently no clear standards about who should get which sorts of treatment and what the outcomes should be. In addition, counsellors and therapists are not registered or regulated. **We will work with the relevant professions to develop standards and work towards light-touch registration that is not unnecessarily burdensome.**

More local focus on health and well-being
2.52 People expect to take responsibility for their health and well-being but they also expect central and local government to play their part by developing services which support them to do this. This starts with local bodies directly based in local communities.

Local leadership

2.53 At the local level, joint action to support health and well-being needs to be driven through strong effective leadership within PCTs and local authorities.

2.54 Our plans to strengthen PCTs will ensure enhanced commissioning for health lies at the heart of their activities. Subject to the outcomes of current local consultations on the proposed reconfiguration of PCTs and SHA boundaries, we expect to see the development of greater co-terminosity between health and local government bodies: both between PCTs and local authorities, and between SHAs and Government Offices for the Regions.

2.55 These changes, to be completed by April 2006, should facilitate better joint working. They need to be backed by strong leadership at chief executive and board level, and by individuals who have clear responsibilities for improving people's health and well-being. Two changes will be central to this.

2.56 Following the creation of the role of the DASS by the Children Act 2004,[18] guidance has been developed to support local authorities to implement this role. We published this as draft best practice guidance alongside *Independence, Well-being and Choice*. There was particularly strong endorsement in the consultation process for the proposed focus for the DASS on co-ordination between agencies such as health, housing and transport to promote social inclusion, alongside the DASS's responsibility for the quality of social care services.

2.57 The proposal for the DASS to play a central role in ensuring that arrangements are in place to support young people during the transition to adult services, working with directors of children's services, was also welcomed. **As a result, it is our intention to issue revised statutory guidance on the role of the DASS, with supporting best practice guidance, during 2006.** Some local authorities and PCTs are appointing joint DASS to support integrated working.

2.58 We will redefine and strengthen the role of the DPH so that public health resources are brought to bear across the public sector to promote health and well-being for the whole community, ensuring a clear and strong focus on tackling health inequalities, alongside the DPH's wider role in protecting health and ensuring clinical safety. In particular, DPHs should ensure that they work closely with local authorities and provide reports directly to local authority overview and scrutiny committees on well-being. Some PCTs and local authorities have already made joint DPH appointments as a mechanism for facilitating this.

2.59 We expect to see more joint appointments of this kind and will promote them in our work to develop the DPH role. Such joint appointments will be most effective in the context of closer co-operation between organisations, for example by using existing flexibilities to form joint teams and shared accountability arrangements as well as moving towards more devolved and joint budgets to improve inter-agency working.

2.60 The DASS and the DPH will play key roles, with directors of children's services, in advising on how local authorities and PCTs will jointly promote the health and well-being of their local communities. They will need to undertake regular joint reviews of the health and well-being status and needs of their populations. They will be responsible for a regular strategic needs assessment to enable local services to plan ahead for the next 10 to 15 years, and to support the development of the wider health and social care market, including services for those who have the ability to pay for social care services themselves. We will include responsibility for leading strategic assessment of needs in the statutory guidance on the DASS.

Better partnership

2.61 Good partnerships are built on common aims.

2.62 Setting clear outcomes for services helps partners to focus on what joint working is aiming to achieve for individuals. *Every Child Matters* has already set five key outcomes for children's services, which are built into Local Area Agreements (LAAs).

2.63 Responses to the consultation on *Independence, Well-being and Choice* strongly supported the proposed outcomes which it set out for adult social care services, based on the concept of well-being. These were:
- improved health and emotional well-being;
- improved quality of life;
- making a positive contribution;
- choice and control;
- freedom from discrimination;
- economic well-being;
- personal dignity.

2.64 These outcomes are important to all of us, whether or not we receive social care services. The Commission for Social Care Inspection (CSCI) is already developing indicators to support these outcomes in social care. **We endorse them as outcomes towards which social care services should be working, with their partners. We will build on them to develop outcomes that apply both to the NHS and social care. We will also use this set of outcomes measures to structure our goal-setting for health, social care and related activity in the LAAs negotiated over the next two years.**

2.65 If we want services to work together to deliver common outcomes, we need to ensure that performance measures for services reinforce and help deliver health and well-being outcomes. The current Public Service Agreement (PSA) targets for local services do include some measures to drive joint work in key areas, for example between the NHS and social care on support for people with long-term conditions, and help for people to be supported at home. But we need to go further to align performance measures. **We will therefore take forward the development of performance assessment regimes to achieve this, reinforced through inspection.**

2.66 Subject to the current wider regulatory review of health and social care arm's-length bodies, we have already made public our aim to merge the Commission for Social Care Inspection with the Healthcare Commission by 2008. As these two organisations join, we will ask them to work together to ensure that their **assessment and inspection arrangements complement each other in support of these outcomes.** They will also continue to work with the Audit Commission to ensure that the relationship between social services and wider local government functions is properly recognised.

2.67 The assessment arrangements will measure how well commissioners ensure delivery against their locally agreed plans to promote health and well-being. This work will be undertaken jointly with our partners across and outside Government, including the Better Regulation Executive and the Audit Commission. It will parallel the current work on a joint inspection framework for children's services.

2.68 Good partnership working requires clarity about what each partner will contribute to joint work towards agreed targets and goals, and mechanisms that help them plan to achieve them. In *Local Strategic Partnerships: Shaping Their Future,*[19] Local Strategic Partnerships (LSPs) are positioned as the 'partnership of partnerships' that draw up Sustainable Community strategies for the economic, social and environmental well-being of their areas. These strategies bring together the views, needs and aspirations of communities and businesses; local service data and trends; and national, regional, local and neighbourhood priorities.

2.69 Sustainable Community strategies set the local priorities for LAAs. LAAs simplify funding streams, targets and reporting arrangements to enable local partners to deliver better public services. LSPs add value by bringing diverse partnerships together with their mainstream and area-based funding to commission services that will deliver the Sustainable Community strategy and LAA.

2.70 Proposals in *Local Strategic Partnerships: Shaping Their Future* are an important part of an ongoing and open debate with local government and other stakeholders on the vision for the future of local government which will be drawn together in the form of a White Paper in summer 2006. Central to this long-term vision are the principles of devolution and decentralisation.

2.71 We believe that LAAs are a key development in helping to achieve good partnership working. They provide a framework for local services including social care and PCTs to deliver improved health and social care outcomes for people in communities, whether provided by public, voluntary or private bodies.

2.72 LAAs are made up of outcomes, indicators and targets aimed at delivering a better quality of life for people by improving performance of local services. LAAs are being rolled out across the country over the next two years. The first 20 pilot agreements were signed in March 2005 and plans are in place for all local authorities to be included by 2006/07. The experience of the current LAA pilots has shown that they have the potential to facilitate integrated service planning and delivery across all those who provide services in a locality. As well as delivering national priorities, they also allow the necessary space for local priorities and can provide an effective way of involving the voluntary and community sectors and the local business community.

2.73 The Office of the Deputy Prime Minister has published a toolkit based on the lessons learnt from these areas and highlighting some of the challenges that will arise as an LAA develops, and how these might be addressed. **We will build on the experience of the LAA pilots to develop them as a key mechanism for joint planning and delivery.**

2.74 At the moment there are practical barriers that get in the way of joint planning to deliver common aims. The different organisations that need to work together to meet these outcomes have different planning and budgeting cycles, created in part by Whitehall. These should be brought in line with each other.

2.75 Therefore, working across departments, the Government will align the planning and budgeting cycle for the NHS with the timetable for local government planning and budget-setting, making a start in 2007/08.

Stronger local commissioning – getting the best out of public resources to improve local people's well-being and independence

2.76 The main responsibility for developing services that improve health and well-being lies with local bodies: PCTs and local authorities. They have a vital role in making sure public resources are used effectively to promote health and well-being and to support high-quality services. This range of functions is generally referred to as 'commissioning' (see paragraphs 1.44–45). Good local commissioning will help local people to stay well and independent and tackle health inequalities.

2.77 In Chapter 7 we set out our proposals for strengthening local commissioning and ensuring that it is more responsive to local needs, as well as our plans for a new joint

Respect: partnership in action

The Government's recently published Respect Action Plan illustrates partnership in action, at the national and local level. Respect is a cross-government programme, led by the Respect Task Force, setting out measures which bear down down on anti-social behaviour, and the wider culture of disrespect within society. Strong partnership between national and local government, between local services and with people and communities is at the heart of the Respect Action Plan. The main aims of the Plan are to:

- support families;
- bring a new approach to dealing with the most challenging families;
- improve behaviour and attendance in schools;

- increase activities for children and young people;
- strengthen communities;
- ensure effective enforcement and community justice.

Health and social care services have key roles to play, working with local partners, in taking forward the Action Plan, including through drug treatment, alcohol and mental health services, and working with other services to deliver better support for children and young people at risk.

"We are committed to providing community-focused health services to address those health problems which cause anti-social behaviour" – Patricia Hewitt, Secretary of State for Health.

commissioning framework covering health and social care services.

The legal framework

2.78 Local bodies' responsibilities are defined in law. One of the three main statutory purposes of a PCTs is to promote the health of its population. Local authorities have the power to promote social and economic well-being, and there are duties on both local authorities and PCTs to co-operate in promoting the well-being of children which were introduced by the Children Act 2004. Local bodies will also be

guided by the statutory obligations under the public sector duties on race, disability (from December 2006) and gender equality (from April 2007) to ensure that service delivery is improved.

2.79 The consultation paper *Local Strategic Partnerships: Shaping Their Future* has already asked for views on whether a duty should be placed on all partners in an LSP to co-operate with local authorities in producing and implementing community strategies. Subject to the outcome of that consultation, we see a strong case

*You can't just deal with the symptoms. You need to get to the root
cause of the problem. This links to big questions like housing.*

PARTICIPANT AT THE CITIZENS' SUMMIT IN BIRMINGHAM

for clarifying the duties on the NHS and local authorities to co-operate in exercising their functions. **We will look carefully at the responses to the consultation when deciding on whether we need to bring forward measures, in addition to those outlined in this White Paper, to strengthen partnership working to support the health and well-being of local communities, and to tackle disadvantage and inequality.**

Shifting the system towards prevention

2.80 In their consultation responses, people told us that they want services not only to support them in maintaining their health and well-being, but to do more to prevent problems.

2.81 Prevention begins by building good health and a healthy lifestyle from the beginning of an individual's life. We are strengthening the provision of antenatal, postnatal and health and early years services, including through our proposals for the new NHS 'Life Check'.

2.82 There is also a growing evidence base showing that preventative measures involving a range of local authority services, such as housing, transport, leisure and community safety, in addition to social care, can achieve significant improvements in well-being. Chapter 6 sets out proposals for shifting resources into prevention.

2.83 Integrated health and social care services, and better links with occupational health advice, can help prevent inappropriate use of specialist or acute health care. For example well-

Figure 2.6 Top prevention ideas from consultation

Routine physical examinations for anyone who wants one
Information, advice and support on monitoring your own cholesterol
Information, advice and support on diet and nutrition
An NHS book on taking care of your own health
Information, advice and support on exercise and physical activity

0 10 20 30 40 50 60 70 80 90 100

■ Likelihood of use*   ■ Perceived relevance

Source: YHYCYS Online Survey
N = 25,666 adjusted and weighted for population
* Likelihood of use for those finding it relevant

Doncaster's Green Gym – where keeping fit is good for the whole community

Keeping fit doesn't have to be about taking up a new sport or going to the swimming pool. Doncaster's Green Gym is a project run by the local PCT and the British Trust for Conservation Volunteers where people can have a healthy workout in the open air and contribute to local conservation work.

Community support worker, Pauline Mitchell, from Thorne Social Education Centre, enjoys getting to the Green Gym almost as much as the people with learning disabilities whom she takes there.

"We've taken a derelict allotment and transformed it – clearing the ground, digging it over, planting the seeds and then watering and feeding them. After their hard work they were thrilled to see the shoots come up and then watch the vegetables grow and be able to harvest them and take them home," says Pauline.

"The Gym offers so many benefits for the people we work with. It's a holistic activity and as well as helping people to get fit, the work gives them the chance to become involved in something for the whole community. They learn about teamwork and develop new skills. They love going out into the countryside and the work provides a real sense of satisfaction and fulfilment."

timed interventions and greater social inclusion can prevent or reduce the severity of episodes of mental illness. Access to appropriate therapy services can reduce the need for people to take time off work, good community services for older people can reduce unplanned admissions to hospital, and well-timed interventions and greater social inclusion can prevent or reduce the severity of episodes of mental illness or homelessness.

2.84 We intend to expand the evidence base through our investment in a number of areas, in particular the Partnerships for Older People Projects (POPPs). Ring-fenced funding of £60 million has already been earmarked for 2006/07 to 2007/08 in order to facilitate a series of pilots.

If I'd got help before, I may not have deteriorated as quickly as I have done.

RESPONDENT TO *INDEPENDENCE, WELL-BEING AND CHOICE*

2.85 Operational from 1 May 2006, the POPPs will provide examples of how innovative partnership arrangements can lead to improved outcomes for older people, particularly with respect to reduced hospital admissions and residential care stays. They bring together a range of interventions, which have been chosen because of their combined potential to provide a sustainable shift of resources and culture towards prevention across the whole health and care system.

2.86 The economic case for primary and secondary disease prevention has been made. The task now is to develop local services that translate this evidence into service delivery.

2.87 The accessibility and use of the evidence base for interventions that support health and well-being will be overseen through a new National Reference Group for Health and Well-being. The National Institute for Health and Clinical Excellence (NICE) and the Social Care Institute for Excellence (SCIE) will play key roles. Building on the *Choosing Health* information strategy, a central database will also be developed as a resource for commissioners.

2.88 In future, healthy living services will be provided by a range of people in different settings including local surgeries, community pharmacies, voluntary sector organisations, leisure/community centres, healthy living centres, sheltered housing, children's centres and schools. Building

on local social capital will help develop community skills and provide employment opportunities across communities that have the greatest needs. Chapter 6 sets out plans for monitoring the development of preventative services in PCTs' local delivery plans.

2.89 Innovative primary care services are already working to identify at-risk patients on their lists and target interventions and advice to them. The new primary medical services contracts include a powerful set of incentives, through the QOF, for practices to identify patients with long-term conditions or lifestyle risk factors such as smoking, and manage their care effectively.

2.90 The QOF now covers 10 disease areas including mental health, diabetes, heart disease, asthma and chronic obstructive pulmonary disorder; and from 2006/07 it will have 7 new areas including obesity, learning difficulty, chronic kidney disease and palliative care. The QOF will drive health improvement in two ways.

2.91 First, practices will be rewarded for managing the care of patients effectively and in line with the best evidence available. **As the QOF evolves we intend that by 2008/09 it will include new measures which provide a clear focus on wider health and well-being outcomes.** The National Reference Group for Health and Well-Being will have a key role in development of the QOF, providing

Fitness friends are FAB

Having a few understanding friends can make a huge difference when you're trying to make some big changes in your life. Fit Active Braunstone (FAB) has around 200 members from the Braunstone housing estate in Leicester, supporting and encouraging each other as they change their lifestyle for the better. Since joining FAB, 42-year-old Gary Buncher has lost four stone, is much fitter and is secretary of FAB's Calorie Killers group.

"Before FAB all I did was go to work, watch telly and have a few beers. I was hugely overweight. Now I swim for two hours five times a week. Every Wednesday evening I go to Calorie Killers, our exercise and nutrition group. We have 45 minutes of exercise and 45 minutes on healthy eating. It's had a big impact – one guy who's diabetic has massively reduced his insulin since joining. We're starting training courses in badminton,

football and basic food hygiene. I've also done a course qualifying me to give nutritional advice to people like diabetics.

"My family says I'm a better person to live with. I feel better about myself and actually enjoy getting up in the mornings."

expert advice to NHS and social care employers who will consult primary care representative groups in the normal way.

2.92 Second, the QOF means that every practice now has a register of patients with long-term needs. These registers provide a clinical database that is unparalleled anywhere else in the world. It is essential that such a unique database is used to improve local

decisions on meeting needs. **We will ensure that commissioning decisions use QOF data about the local population.**

The Quality and Outcomes Framework leads to better care for patients

While only one year of data exists, the QOF has been an undoubted success. Quality scores have hit 958 points on average out of 1050, that is, over 91 per cent achievement.

Coronary heart disease

- 1.5 million people with coronary heart disease (CHD) had their blood pressure managed at the clinically acceptable level of 150/90 or less;

- 1.2 million people with CHD had their cholesterol levels managed at the clinically acceptable level of 5 mmol/l or less;

- 1.8 million people with both CHD and lower ventricular dysfunction were bring treated with ACE inhibitors (or A2 antagonists).

Stroke

- almost 600,000 stroke patients had their blood pressure managed at a clinically acceptable level of 150/90 or less;

- 410,000 stroke patients had their cholesterol levels managed to a clinically acceptable level of 5 mmol/l or less;

- over 565,000 stroke patients had a flu jab.

High blood pressure

- 5.4 million people with hypertension had their blood pressure monitored in the previous 9 months;

- 4 million people with hypertension had their blood pressure managed at a clinically acceptable level of 150/90 or less.

Asthma

- 2.1 million people with asthma had a review in the previous 15 months;

- 1.3 million people with asthma had a flu jab.

Diabetes

- 1.4 million people with diabetes had retinal screening in the previous 15 months;

- 1.7 million people with diabetes had their blood pressure monitored in the previous 15 months;

- 1.2 million people with diabetes had their blood pressure managed at a clinically acceptable level of 145/85 or less;

- 1.1 million people with diabetes had their cholesterol levels managed to a clinically acceptable level of 5 mmol/l or less;

- 1.3 million people with diabetes had a flu jab.

Chronic obstructive pulmonary disease (COPD)

- over 555,000 patients with COPD had a flu jab.

Epilepsy

- over 172,000 patients on drug treatment for epilepsy had been convulsion free for the previous 12 months.

Social prescribing

2.93 Chapter 5 sets out our proposals for introducing information prescriptions for them with long-term conditions, to enable them to access a wider provision of services. A range of different 'prescription' schemes, such as exercise-on-prescription projects, have been established or piloted in a number of areas and have often been very successful.

2.94 We would like to see increasing uptake of well-being prescriptions by PCTs and their local partners, aimed at promoting good health and independence and ensuring people have easy access to a wide range of services, facilities and activities.

National leadership

2.95 The Government has a responsibility to promote leadership for health and well-being across and between different services. This chapter has concentrated so far on our proposals to support individuals to take care of their own health and well-being, and to revise the framework within which local services work, in order to drive stronger local partnership working.

2.96 To offer strong leadership to a more integrated system we also need to work much more closely together in Whitehall than previously. We have already identified a number of areas, including the development of LAAs,

where work will be taken forwards through strong collaboration.

2.97 The Department of Health performs a leadership function in relation to the health and social care systems. It has recently undertaken a review of its structure and during the spring will be working to develop a more integrated approach to this leadership role. **In particular, we will make a new appointment to the Department of Health's Board focusing on social care. We will develop a more detailed specification for this position, with a view to making a substantive appointment by July 2006.**

2.98 *Choosing Health* described a comprehensive framework for action across Government in England to enable people to make healthy choices. Since its publication, London has been awarded the honour of staging the 2012 Olympic Games. This will provide a unique opportunity to work closely with the devolved administrations to promote a fitter Britain.

2.99 The Department of Health will work with partner organisations, including Sport England and the London Olympic Games Organising Committee, to maximise opportunities for people to take part in recreational and health-promoting activities. **A high-profile campaign, building on the health strategies in England, Scotland, Wales and Northern Ireland, will be developed, encouraging everyone to contribute to the drive for a fitter Britain by 2012.**

A focus on both physical and emotional health will be part of this drive for fitness, which will be inclusive of all age groups.

References

1   House of Commons Health Committee, *Obesity: 3rd report of session 2003–04*: (HC 23-1), The Stationery Office, 2004

2   *Who cares wins: Absence and labour turnover 2005*. Confederation of British Industry, 2005

3   (i) Derek Wanless, *Securing Our Future Health: Taking a Long-Term View*, Interim Report, HM Treasury, November 2001; (ii) Derek Wanless, *Securing Our Future Health: Taking a Long-Term View*, Final Report, HM Treasury, April 2002

4   *Every Child Matters* (Cm 6499), The Stationery Office, September 2003

5   *National Service Framework for Children, Young People and Maternity Services*, Department of Health, September 2004

6   Evidence from the National Foundation for Educational Research has shown that 40 per cent of pupils lose motivation and make no progress in the year after transfer to secondary school. The precise reasons for this are unclear, although many of those directly involved in the crucial transition years report similar concerns. Communication difficulties, cultural differences between the primary and secondary 'styles' and insufficient attention to the emotions of changing schools crop up as possible causes time and again. See: http://www.teachernet.gov.uk/teaching andlearning/library/transitionphase/

7   *Support for parents: the best start for children*, HM Treasury and Department for Education and Skills, December 2005

8   *Youth Matters*, Green Paper (Cm 6629), The Stationery Office, July 2005

9   *Health, work and well-being – caring for our future*, Department for Work and Pensions, Department of Health and Health and Safety Executive, October 2005

10 *Opportunity Age – Opportunity and security throughout life*, Department for Work and Pensions, March 2005

11 *A Sure Start to Later Life: Ending Inequalities for Older People*, A Social Exclusion Unit Final Report, Office of the Deputy Prime Minister, January 2006

12 *Improving the life chances of disabled people*, joint report, Prime Minister's Strategy Unit, Department for Work and Pensions, Department of Health, Department for Education and Skills, and Office of the Deputy Prime Minister, January 2005

13 *Creating Sustainable Communities: Supporting Independence*, Office of the Deputy Prime Minister, November 2005

14 *Effective Health Care. Cholesterol and coronary heart disease: screening and treatment*, vol 4 (no 1), University of York, NHS Centre for Reviews and Dissemination, 1988: 1–16

15 *Health Survey for England 2004*. Target: a minimum of five days a week of 30 minutes or more moderate-intensity activity

16 HealthSpace is an on-line service provided by the NHS for patients in England. For more information see: https://www.healthspace.nhs.uk/ index.asp

17 *Making it possible: Improving mental health and well-being*, National Institute for Mental Health in England and Care Services Improvement Partnership, October 2005

18 Schedule 2 of the 2004 Children Act removed the duty on local authorities in England to appoint a Director of Social Services and a Chief Education Officer. It also amended the duty to appoint a Director of Social Services under section 6 of the Local Authority Social Services Act 1970, so that CSAs in England are now required to appoint a DASS

19 *Local Strategic Partnerships: Shaping Their Future*, consultation paper, Office of the Deputy Prime Minister, December 2005

CHAPTER 3

Better access to general practice

Better access to general practice

This chapter on primary care services includes:

- helping people register with the GP practice of their choice;
- rewarding responsive providers;
- increasing provision in deprived areas: supporting Primary Care Trusts (PCTs) to attract new providers;
- helping practices to expand by helping with expansion costs and making more money follow the patient;
- reviewing the funding of NHS Walk-in Centres;
- giving people more information on local services;
- new drive to improve the availability and quality of primary care provision in areas of deprivation, so that problems of health inequality and worklessness can be tackled.

Introduction

3.1 When people are asked about their local NHS, they probably think first of their GP. For the last 60 years, GPs have played a vital role in the NHS, acting as the main service provider, first point of contact for most people and the 'gatekeeper' to other services. These have always included hospital care and access to social security benefits aimed at helping people with sickness or disability.

3.2 Increasingly, however, a GP-led practice will also involve nurse practitioners and practice nurses and may include other healthcare professionals, such as physiotherapists, drug and alcohol counsellors, mental health counsellors, and therapists. In the future, there may also be specialists to give advice on employment aspects of being sick or disabled.

3.3 At one end of the spectrum is the small practice, owned and run by one or two GPs, possibly assisted by a practice nurse. At the other end is the very large practice – perhaps itself part of an integrated health and social care centre – with a full team of GPs, nurses, therapists and other professionals. New models are also developing, including NHS Walk-in Centres and a few primary care practices that are led by nurse practitioners, with a salaried GP available for those cases requiring a GP's particular skills. In this chapter, therefore, we refer to 'primary care practices' as well as 'GP practices'.

3.4 Access to high-quality primary healthcare has a vital role in helping people to live longer and healthier lives. Integration of these services with other community and social care services helps to ensure better co-ordinated support and care for each individual, better management of chronic disease, and reduced need for costly and avoidable hospital care. General practice remains best placed to offer patients their usual point of contact for routine and continuing care, and to help patients to navigate other parts of the system.

3.5 By international standards, general practice in England is efficient and of high quality.[1] Indeed, many countries view with envy our system of list-based general practice and some, for example Spain, have sought to copy it.

3.6 We implemented major reforms to primary healthcare in 2003/04. These reforms have been backed by an unprecedented increase in resources. By the end of 2005/06, investment in primary medical care services in England will have increased by well over £2 billion compared with financial year 2002/03. This investment underpins a system of incentives aimed at expanding the range of services provided in general practice, rewarding improvements in clinical quality and patient experience and recruiting and retention of key professionals.

3.7 These reforms are delivering. As a result of the hard work and dedication of around 160,000 GPs, nurses and others working in and alongside general practice, primary care is now delivering better quality than ever before; and a wider range of specialist services are available. We have recruited 3,950 more GPs since publication of the *NHS Plan*,[2] including over 2,700 since March 2003 when the contractual changes came into place. Job satisfaction has increased and our GPs are now among the best paid in the world.

3.8 However, while public satisfaction with the services they receive in primary care is generally high, this varies across the country.[3] Services do not always respond to the needs of local communities and individuals, for example by providing services that are appropriate to particular black and minority ethnic groups, nor do they reflect high levels of deprivation. There is also marked variation in how easy people find it to telephone their practice and make a convenient appointment. Access for some people remains difficult in some circumstances.

3.9 In order to improve access and responsiveness we need to put people more in control. If the public could genuinely choose their practice, their needs and preferences would have more impact on shaping services. We need, therefore, to make real the choices that people should have and reward existing practices and other new providers who respond to those choices.

3.10 To ensure that the NHS value of equal access for all is a reality, we must also do more to improve access and build up capacity in poorly served areas. While many people can choose between several high-quality practices, others find there is only one practice in their area with whom they can register. Particular groups of people, such as care home residents, people with learning disabilities, and people who are homeless or living in temporary accommodation, often have great difficulty in finding a GP at all.

3.11 In some places this will mean encouraging or allowing new providers, including social enterprises or commercial companies, to offer services to registered patients alongside traditional general practice. Increased capacity – and contestability – will allow people to choose services that offer more convenient opening times, tailored specialist services or co-location with other relevant services.

Making it easier to register with an open practice

3.12 Since 1948 patients have had the right to choose their GP and primary healthcare provider. This right to choose to register with a practice is a fundamental building block of the NHS:

- it is part of the public's basic right to access their NHS;
- it establishes the right to care from patients' chosen practice, supports continuity of care and forms the basis from which practices take responsibility for the wider public health of their registered population;
- it also provides the foundation for the allocation of NHS expenditure across England on a fair basis according to the needs of the local population.

3.13 For most people, choosing a general practice is one of their most important and personal health care decisions:

- on average, each person sees their GP four times a year. When practice nurses, counsellors and other staff are included, this amounts to over 300 million consultations in primary care each year. Fifteen per cent of the population sees a GP in any two-week period;[4]
- 75 per cent of people have been with their general practice for longer than five years;
- nearly one in three people have a long-term condition. People with a long-term condition particularly value continuity of care by someone who understands their problems and whom they know and trust.

3.14 Levels of satisfaction with general practice are consistently high. Yet we know that – for some – problems persist. At times, these problems materially restrict the ability of individuals to register with a practice of their choice.

3.15 Some people, for example, would like to change their practice to another one. This seems a relatively simple right for a member of the public paying for their services through taxation to carry out. Yet it can be difficult to do.

3.16 There is not always good, accessible information on practices and what they offer.[5] There are not always practices available that are 'open' to new registrations – that is, taking on new patients. This needs to be put right.

3.17 Other people would like the option of being able to register with a practice near to where they work, rather than where they live. At the moment many practices do not take on new patients who live outside the geographical catchment area that the practice agrees with its PCT (and which defines the area in which the practice is required to make home visits where there is a clinical need).

3.18 All these factors mean that at present choice of practice in primary care is too often more of a theoretical proposition than a practical reality. We will put this right. We will ensure that PCTs (as commissioners), practices and new providers respond to the choices and needs of the public as the best way of driving service improvements – not to exhortation from Whitehall.

3.19 We have also considered whether patients should be allowed to register with more than one practice at the same time, increasing convenience, particularly for commuters. This is known as 'dual registration'. However, this approach would undermine the underlying principles of registration, including continuity of care, and would be difficult and costly to introduce. Nor did this approach receive support during the *Your health, your care, your say* listening exercise, ranking seventh among options presented in the questionnaire. We are already introducing a range of policies designed to enhance access.

3.20 NHS Walk-in Centres already provide easy access to a range of primary care services to all patients on demand. A new wave of NHS Walk-in Centres in commuter areas are beginning to open. These services should continue to be developed according to local needs, to ensure that people who lead busy lives have equal access to NHS services. For all these reasons we are ruling out dual registration.

Tackling closed lists

3.21 Registration will continue as the cornerstone of list-based general

practice. However, we need to ensure that the right to register is a reality for all. **In future, patients will be guaranteed acceptance onto an open list in their locality and we will review how we can simplify the process for doing so.** Only in exceptional cases of abuse (for example violence) by patients will this not apply.

3.22 We will also simplify the handling of 'closed' lists. Although only 3 per cent of practices report operating closed lists, many more are 'open but full' – in other words, although they are not formally closed, the practice does not usually accept new registrations. This makes it harder for patients to find a convenient local practice, particularly in areas with low levels of primary care provision. It also inhibits choice and transparency and fails to safeguard against discrimination.

3.23 The existing closed list procedures will be made simpler to operate, in order to provide greater transparency for patients and to offer practices the flexibility they need to manage short-term or longer-term capacity issues. Practices will operate either an open list or a closed list. These changes will ensure that patients choose practices, not the reverse.

3.24 Linked with this, we will clarify the rules on eligibility and streamline the process for patients to register. We will make the access rules more transparent and make the registration process simpler for patients and providers.

3.25 There will be an obligation on PCTs to provide up-to-date, authoritative information to the public on whether a practice is open for new patients, the range of services it provides, its opening hours and so on. We will make it easier for everyone to get the information they need to choose a practice, including via the internet.

Making it easier for responsive practices to expand

3.26 In order to give people more choice of the practice they want, we need to ensure that popular practices benefit from taking on new patients. There are two main barriers:

- the costs of taking on new patients are not fully reflected in the current contract for GP services – money does not follow the patient;
- practices that do want to expand are not helped to do so.

3.27 Our approach is to ensure that there is an effective set of incentives in place that will deliver what patients need and expect. Rewarding responsive providers is the best way to ensure that patients' needs are taken into account.

3.28 The way we invest in general practice goes some way towards ensuring money is allocated on the basis of need and that it follows the patient. However, less than 70 per cent

Figure 3.1 General practice contract types

General medical services	Personal medical services	Alternative provider of medical services	Primary Care Trust medical services
• Nationally agreed contract between the Department of Health (or bodies acting on behalf of the Department of Health) and the British Medical Association. • Recent negotiations led to an overhaul of the contract, which included practice-based rather than GP-based payments, stronger quality incentives, and more flexibility to increase range of services provided.	• Alternative to GMS, in which the contract is agreed locally between the practice and the PCT. • Designed to encourage local flexibility and innovation and a focus on local population needs. • Many of the developments in the new GMS contract have also been adopted in PMS.	• Route for provision of primary medical services where PCT may contract with the independent sector, voluntary sector, not-for-profit organisations, NHS Trusts, other PCTs, Foundation Trusts, or even GMS and PMS practices.	• PCT-provided medical services. • Route to provision of primary medical services where PCT employs the GPs, nurses and others in the primary health care team. • Has been used as a lever for providing care where it has not proved possible to attract GPs to open practices.

Source: Department of Health

of payments to practices on the national contract transfer with a patient when they move, and local Personal Medical Services (PMS) arrangements are open to local negotiation. In addition, premises funding stays with the original practice and most General Medical Services (GMS) practices are protected by a Minimum Practice Income Guarantee (MPIG). This was introduced to ensure that practices did not face a fall in income in moving to the new GMS contract in 2004. This reduction in income has not happened – indeed, most practice incomes have risen substantially.

3.29 One of the aims of both the PMS and GMS was to invest in practices and their populations based on patient need.

3.30 For GMS, a review of the funding formula is due to report in time for implementation in 2007/08. This will inform the next round of discussions between NHS Employers and the General Practice Committee (GPC). On the back of the substantial additional investment in general practice between 2003 and 2007, and a need to have more money following the patient, we will also ask NHS Employers to consider the MPIG and its impact on equity when discussing incentives for 2007/08 and beyond.

3.31 We will also undertake a fundamental review of the financial arrangements for the 40 per cent of practices on local PMS contracts. Many have developed innovative new services.

CASE STUDY

Innovative GP services

The James Wigg Practice in Kentish Town – an inner-city London neighbourhood with high levels of disadvantage and health inequalities – is demonstrating the range of services that can be provided by primary care. The practice has GPs and nurses, of course, but it offers so much more.

Visiting specialists include an alcohol counsellor, a drug counsellor, an adult psychologist and psychiatrist, an ophthalmologist and a rheumatologist. Clinics are run by practice nurses for many ongoing conditions, including diabetes, asthma, hypertension and quitting smoking.

The practice makes extensive use of information techology. This means that patients can order repeat prescriptions using the internet. This emphasis on information technology has led to the practice being awarded beacon status. Patients can also conduct telephone consultations with doctors if they need advice or want to ascertain if they need to make an appointment.

3.32 However, providers are not always rewarded for attracting new patients to take advantage of innovative services. We would like all practices – whatever their contract type – to have a real incentive to take on new patients, where this is what people choose.

3.33 The second barrier to practices expanding are the steep extra costs. We will ask NHS Employers to consider the case for establishing an Expanding Practice Allowance for practices that have open lists which are growing significantly and that offer extended opening hours. Aside from such developments, we will expect PCTs to prioritise expanding practices when allocating strategic capital monies.

3.34 We will also review the arrangements for funding NHS Walk-in Centres and for paying for services provided by general practice to unregistered patients. The aim will be to ensure that all providers have the right incentives to deliver care to patients while away from their registered practice.

3.35 PCTs' existing duty to inform local residents of the services available will be extended to include information on the establishment of new services and expanding practices. This will mean that the public are better informed about the choices open to them.

Health inequalities

3.36 These changes will make registration easier for most. But there are persistent and particular problems in deprived areas which have long been under-served.[6] We intend to increase provision in areas that are not well served – which are typically the most needy areas – to increase the equity of provision and to ensure that everyone has a real choice.

Figure 3.2 Bottom 10 per cent of PCTs with the fewest doctors

Rank	PCT	GPs (WTE) per 100,000 weighted population	Spear-head PCT
1	NORTH MANCHESTER PCT	40.6	S
2	WYRE PCT	43.2	
3	ASHFIELD PCT	43.6	
4	TRAFFORD NORTH PCT	43.8	
5	SWALE PCT	43.8	
6	OLDHAM PCT	44.0	S
7	MANSFIELD DISTRICT PCT	44.1	
8	DONCASTER WEST PCT	44.2	S
9	WALSALL PCT	44.3	S
10	KNOWSLEY PCT	44.5	S
11	WOLVERHAMPTON CITY PCT	44.7	S
12	DONCASTER EAST PCT	45.0	S
13	ASHTON, LEIGH AND WIGAN PCT	45.1	S
14	BURNLEY, PENDLE AND ROSSENDALE PCT	45.1	S
15	BARKING AND DAGENHAM PCT	45.2	S

Rank	PCT	GPs (WTE) per 100,000 weighted population	Spear-head PCT
16	BLACKPOOL PCT	45.3	S
17	NORTH STOKE PCT	45.5	S
18	EASTERN HULL PCT	45.5	S
19	WEDNESBURY AND WEST BROMWICH PCT	45.7	S
20	TENDRING PCT	46.3	
21	BARNSLEY PCT	46.4	S
22	EASINGTON PCT	46.5	S
23	SHEPWAY PCT	46.5	
24	HASTINGS AND ST LEONARDS PCT	46.7	
25	NORTH KIRKLEES PCT	46.9	
26	SOUTHPORT AND FORMBY PCT	47.3	
27	SOUTH TYNESIDE PCT	47.4	S
28	OLDBURY AND SMETHWICK PCT	47.5	S
29	HARTLEPOOL PCT	47.5	S
30	BLACKBURN WITH DARWEN PCT	47.5	S

Source: Department of Health Publications and Statistics, Press Releases and Statistics: Reid announces 'Spearhead' PCTs to tackle health inequalities, 19/11/2004, Department of Health General and Personal Medical Services Statistics

Figure 3.3 Under-doctored areas across England

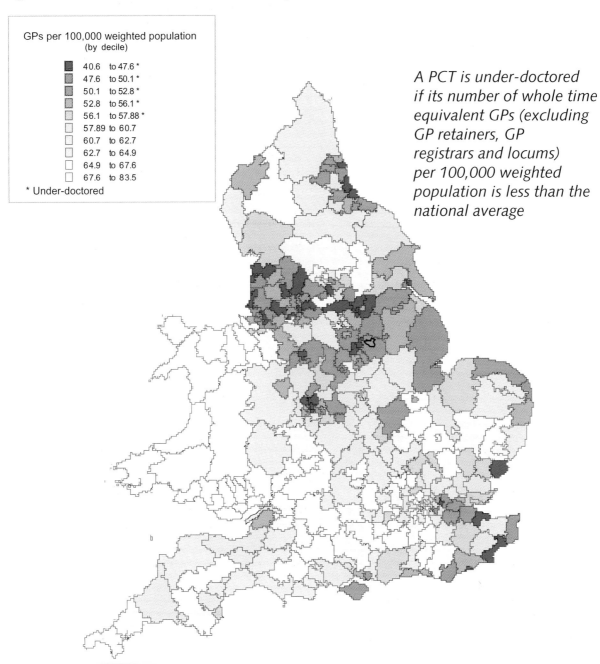

GPs per 100,000 weighted population
(by decile)

■	40.6 to 47.6 *
▨	47.6 to 50.1 *
▨	50.1 to 52.8 *
▨	52.8 to 56.1 *
▨	56.1 to 57.88 *
□	57.89 to 60.7
□	60.7 to 62.7
□	62.7 to 64.9
□	64.9 to 67.6
□	67.6 to 83.5

* Under-doctored

A PCT is under-doctored if its number of whole time equivalent GPs (excluding GP retainers, GP registrars and locums) per 100,000 weighted population is less than the national average

Source: Department of Health General and Personal Medical Services Statistics, March 2005

3.37 The distribution of general practice has been uneven since the beginning of the NHS. Research also shows that those areas with poorest health outcomes are also those with the fewest GPs.[7] The variation is quite large. The PCTs that had the most GPs per 100,000 weighted population had more than double that of the least.

3.38 GPs are one indicator of capacity. There has been a change in emphasis in delivery of primary care, with more team-based approaches involving nurses and other professionals. Although there have been improvements in the overall number of primary care professionals, there has been no significant narrowing of inequalities in provision. Areas with insufficient provision tend to have below average health outcomes and lower levels of patient satisfaction.

3.39 Increasing the quantity and quality of primary health care in the areas of greatest need is one of the most important ways in which this Government can tackle health inequalities. It can improve services for all, so as to guarantee universal access to high-quality primary care services across all parts of the country, appropriate to the local population, and based on need. The issue of quality in primary care is considered further in Chapter 8.

3.40 Part of the new contract deal endorsed by GPs was the creation of new contractual freedoms for PCTs to bring in additional provision (see Figure 3.1). In the next stage of reform these freedoms will be used systematically to reduce inequality in primary care provision.

3.41 On their own, PCTs have not always had the size or clout to develop enough new provision in their locality to tackle inequalities. The Department of Health is currently assisting six PCTs in procuring services from a diverse set of suppliers for communities that have previously been poorly served. Now we will help **all** PCTs in under-served areas to draw upon national expertise to attract new providers of sufficient size to fill these gaps in provision.

3.42 We will do this by ensuring that PCTs actively commission additional practices, reflecting the needs and expectations of their local populations. Change will be driven locally, with local authority input, and co-ordinated nationally in a series of procurement waves. This is an urgent priority if we are to make equal access for equal need a reality.

3.43 We will ensure that both new and existing providers are allowed to provide services in underserved areas. Social enterprises, the voluntary sector and independent sector providers will all make valuable contributions in the longstanding challenge of addressing inequalities. The voluntary and community sectors often have strengths and experience in delivering services to those people who are not well served by traditional services. This will be the basis of the new Fairness in Primary Care procurement principles.

3.44 PCTs will retain full control of their proposed contract specifications, in order to ensure services are tailored to meet local needs, and they will, of course, be responsible for awarding and signing contracts.

3.45 The first wave of nationally supported procurements must address those areas with the most significant inequalities of access to primary care. The Department of Health will assist health communities with the poorest levels of general practice provision. Future waves will be shaped more broadly around the ongoing needs of local populations, ie based on the trigger mechanisms outlined in Chapter 7. They will take into account the broader set of measures, such as patient surveys, patient assignments, closed lists, and unresponsive services. We will ensure that local authorities have the opportunity to input into relevant tender specifications.

New providers in primary care services

The current small business model of GP partnerships is likely to remain very popular. To complement this, larger organisations can bring capital and new management techniques to deliver innovative solutions, such as larger one-stop shop primary care centres, offering a wider range of services, including diagnostics and minor surgery, and convenient opening hours. Some examples include:

Entrepreneurial GPs or nurse practitioners forming large organisations

The organisations would continue as providers under GMS and PMS contracts, however they would be organised into larger units, or be based around networks, allowing the pooling of resources and the delivery of a broader set of services. Practice Based Commissioning is likely to be the prime driver for practices working more closely together.

Co-operatives

There are already 20 GP out-of-hours co-operatives, known as 'mutuals'. Mutuals are not-for-profit organisations where members are entrusted with their social ownership and governance. They can be large enough to enjoy economies of scale and have long-term horizons, yet maintain a local responsive touch in the delivery of patient care. **Mutuo** is leading the development of such organisations. Some out-of-hours co-operatives may be interested in providing a round-the-clock service, based at one or more primary care practices.

Independent sector

The for-profit corporate sector has just begun to provide services in primary care via the use of the Alternative Providers of Medical Services contract. More broadly, **Boots** are offering chlamydia testing in some high street stores in London, and a number of organisations will run commuter-focused Walk-in Centres close to train stations, on behalf of NHS patients.

Mercury Health Primary Care (the primary care arm of an independent sector organisation) has formed a strategic alliance with **Chilvers** and **McCrea**, a company established four years ago by an NHS nurse and a GP, with 18 general medical practices in England. The alliance brings together the size and capital of a corporate body with the specialist expertise of a small entrepreneurial organisation. Mercury also has an affiliation with Frome Medical Practice, one of the largest in the country with 29 GPs.

3.46 The approach to the first wave of the Fairness in Primary Care procurement principles is as follows:

First wave of Fairness in Primary Care procurement principles

1. The Department of Health will begin immediately to identify the localities that are significantly under-provided, especially those in deprived areas.

2. Where PCTs are unable to provide robust plans for rapidly reducing inequalities of access to services, they will be invited to join the national procurement process.

3. There will be a competitive tendering process, which will provide a level playing field and ensure fairness. PCTs will purchase and contract manage the new services.

4. PCTs will draw up specifications for the new services they will procure. These must include arrangements for convenient opening hours, open lists, a practice boundary, if any, very broadly defined, as well as quality incentives comparable to those in the GMS/PMS contract.

5. The Department of Health will manage the procurement process on behalf of PCTs, ensuring the principles of contestability and value for money are realised under a fair, transparent and consistent process.

6. All providers that pre-qualify to quality standards during the tendering process will be put on an accredited list of primary care suppliers, to ensure that in the future commissioners can procure GP services faster.

It's not about making hours 'longer' but making them 'different'. For example, we don't need both morning and afternoon openings, as people who can come in the morning can also come in the afternoon. That way you don't need to stretch the resources.

PARTICIPANT AT THE CITIZENS' SUMMIT IN BIRMINGHAM

Making it easier to get care at the right time

3.47 Registration is not an end in itself. Registration ensures free access to a primary care professional and is the gateway to other services. We want people to register with a practice that provides them with the care that they want. Once a patient is registered, when they need to see a primary care professional, they expect to be seen at a convenient time and quickly.

3.48 The *NHS Plan* set a target of patients being able to see a practice nurse within 24 hours and a GP within 48 hours. This target has led to significant improvements in access to primary care and largely ended the problem of people waiting a week or more to see a GP.

3.49 But it has created new problems. A growing minority of practices stopped offering advance bookings. This is a particular problem for people who want to organise their time ahead or whose need is less urgent.[8] It assumes that the public's time is free. Action has been taken to address this and the problem is diminishing, but more needs to be done.

3.50 The public, quite reasonably, expects both to be able to see a primary care practitioner quickly, and to have the opportunity to book an appointment in advance. *Your health, your care, your say* showed that this is a high priority.

3.51 In response to *Your health, your care, your say*, we have agreed with the British Medical Association (BMA) a new general practice contract framework for 2006/07 that already makes progress on ensuring better access. It sets practices objectives to offer patients:
- the opportunity to consult a GP within 48 hours;
- the opportunity to book appointments in advance;
- easy telephone access;
- the opportunity for the patient to consult their preferred practitioner (while recognising that this may mean waiting longer).

3.52 It is our intention to ensure that people have both the ability to get fast access when they need it and to book ahead. We will use our contracts to deliver this, together with public information on practices not complying, to enable people to make informed choices.

3.53 PCTs will be expected to provide information to all patients on the performance of all practices in an area in offering fast access and advanced booking. This information will list other local practices that are open to new registrations and are meeting the target fully. This will enable them to make informed decisions about the care and services they are receiving.

Smart practices in Lincolnshire

The Hereward Practice in Bourne is one of a number of practices in Lincolnshire that are making use of technology to improve access to services in a predominantly rural area. People registered with the practice can order their prescriptions on-line to collect from chemists the next day, can book their GP appointments using the internet and can sign in using a 'virtual receptionist' when they arrive for an appointment.

People can also access their own patient information easily from a touch-screen in the practice. Fingerprint technology is used to ensure people's records remain secure.

"It's early days at the moment," as Bob Brown, who helped develop the system, explained. "We've got 800 out of 10,000 patients registered and we need to get information out to them about the system and how to use it. We also need to make sure they are confident that their records are secure."

Nevertheless the practice has bold ambitions for the future. "We're also hoping to develop the system so people will be able to use the touch-screens to 'choose and book'." continued Bob. "They will be able to find out which hospitals are available for them for the particular treatment they need, take a look at the hospital on the computer and even the doctor or consultant they are seeing!"

These innovations are just the start. In the future, the practice is seeking to tailor information played on a plasma screen in the waiting area to the people who are there. So if a diabetic signs in with the virtual receptionist, then information on controlling blood sugar could be played in the waiting area.

Ensuring practices are open when the public wants

3.54 Ensuring that services are open when the public want to use them is fundamental to improving access. It was one of their highest priorities in the *Your health, your care, your say* listening exercise. We will tackle this with the professions through a variety of means.

3.55 At present, practices set their own surgery opening hours and have the ability to change these without PCT agreement. There are few incentives to offer opening times that respond to the needs of patients. We will change this.

3.56 First, it will be easier for people to choose which practice they register with. This will enable them to choose practices that offer access that fits with their lives. Practices that offer opening

Figure 3.4 Public views on access

Your health, your care, your say questionnaire: "How much of an improvement would each of these options be for you when you want to see a professional?"

■ Big improvement   ■ Biggest improvement

Source: *Your health, your care, your say* questionnaire
n=25,666 number lowered when weighted for population

hours that the public want will gain new patients, and the money that follows them; those that don't, won't.

3.57 Second, we will directly ask the public how easy it is to get into their practice to see a GP and will reward those whose patients are satisfied. From this year, practice patient surveys, which will be standardised and independently conducted, will ask registered practice populations whether their surgery offers convenient opening hours, including an early morning, evening or Saturday surgery.

3.58 Third, in the future, opening hours should reflect patient preferences and will be agreed with PCTs. We will seek to use the various primary care

Opening longer for patients

People told us that more convenient opening hours was the most important thing for us to tackle to improve access to GPs. They also told us that they didn't want this to mean that staff simply worked longer hours. From late November 2004, two practices in Waltham Forest, North London, piloted extended opening hours to meet their patients' needs. They also restructured staff working hours and engaged additional staff. Here's how it feels for both their patients and people working at one of the practices.

Neil Collins, a 64-year-old retired social worker, has been a patient at Forest Road Medical Centre for three years. "The longer hours scheme was piloted at my surgery for six months last year. I think it could have been advertised a bit better, but once I found out about it, it was great. I found the flexibility very useful and it meant there were more appointments, so it was easier to get to see the doctor at a time that was convenient. For example, one Friday evening I had what I thought was an infected foot. Previously, if this had happened on a Friday night, I would not have been able to get an appointment before Monday and I'd have had to go to the Walk-in Centre or Accident and Emergency. This time I was able to ring and get an appointment for Saturday. I'm also a mental health services user and I suffer from an anxiety disorder, so I tend to worry more about certain things and the flexibility of the appointment system also helped to ease my anxiety, because I knew I could get an appointment if I needed it."

Dr Dinesh Kapoor, a GP at Grange Park Practice, said his patients reacted very positively. "They were so pleased that we were no longer saying 'Sorry, there are no appointments for two weeks' but rather, 'You want to be seen? Come now!' The new system also enabled the practice to increase the length of appointments so, as Dr Kapoor explained, "patients were getting around 50 per cent more time. Immediate access and a longer consultation time with the doctor or nurse were obviously beneficial, particularly for those suffering from chronic diseases.

"The Saturday morning service was particularly popular and it meant that fewer of our practice patients were turning up at the out-of-hours services in the local hospitals. So it contributed to saving costs at the A&E and NHS Walk-in Centres. I believe some patients have transferred to our practice as a result of the scheme."

contracts to provide more incentives for new and existing providers to offer better opening hours.

3.59 Fourth, PCTs will also ensure convenient opening hours across a range of other alternatives. These alternatives include:

- bringing in new providers offering more convenient opening hours (see paragraph 3.46);
- allowing out-of-hours providers to do evening surgeries, take booked appointments and take on registered patients;
- developing new NHS Walk-in Centres and allowing existing sites to take booked appointments.

Choosing **your** primary care professional

3.60 Patients also want to be able to see the GP of their choice within the practice. Women often prefer to see a female GP. Relationship continuity is very important. It is better for both the patient and practitioner if the patient's history and needs are shared and understood, particularly if the patient has ongoing needs.[9]

3.61 Research also shows that where a practitioner has an ongoing professional relationship with a particular patient, they tend to be more committed to the patient as a person.[10] This is one of the reasons why small practices are popular and will remain an essential part of general practice.

3.62 At present, patients can state their preferred GP. If a particular GP is especially popular, this will inevitably mean that the patient cannot see them within 48 hours. It will then be for the patient to decide whether to wait, or instead to see a different GP within 48 hours.

3.63 The public does not always want to see a GP. At the national Citizens' Summit in Birmingham in 2005, over 40 per cent of people picked having a trained nurse as a first point of contact in primary care as one of their top three priorities. We will encourage existing practices and new providers – particularly through the review of urgent care services – to make best use of the first contact skills of nurses. In addition, NHS Walk-in Centres and NHS Direct are already offering this option and the further expansion and development of these services will extend this.

Innovative approaches to access

Nurse triage, perhaps using the telephone, has the potential to reduce pressure on GPs while enabling people to talk to a clinician straight away. We will encourage primary care practices to explore the potential of both nurse triage and telephone consultations, particularly if a practice's survey reveals support for these innovations.

Technology could improve access in primary care. Use of the internet could be made for the booking of GP appointments, for ordering prescriptions from GPs on-line and even, potentially, for registering with a practice on-line. We would encourage practices to explore the potential for technology to improve access and we will work with NHS Connecting for Health on the practicalities for this, as well as learning from examples of best practice.

3.64 As well as increasing the accessibility of GPs and nurses, it is important that access to other primary care professionals is improved where waiting lists exist, such as access to allied health professionals. While many services already operate a self-referral system where patients can access these services themselves without the need to see a doctor, we will be piloting this approach with a comprehensive evaluation (see Chapter 4).

Choosing services that reflect your needs

3.65 If the public has a choice of practices, then those that offer the most appropriate and responsive services will attract more patients. Practices will have to identify and meet the cultural and demographic needs of the population they serve – they will have to design services around the user in order to attract them.

3.66 Some practices will wish to expand and take on more patients outside their current boundaries, thereby increasing choice. In these circumstances they will continue to be free to agree a larger area with their PCT. Other practices or providers may, however, prefer to concentrate on delivering high-quality services to their existing patients or list size.

3.67 We also expect that some existing practices will wish to combine extended boundaries and extended opening hours for maximum coverage for people. We will expect new providers in particular to offer this option to patients.

3.68 PCTs will work closely with their local authority partners to ensure that the associated social care implications of different practice boundaries are taken into account.

3.69 Responsive primary care practices should work within an integrated set of community and local services. In the next chapter we will look at the wider set of services with which primary care practices link.

References

1   Starfield B. *Primary care: balancing health needs, services and technology*, Oxford University Press, 1998

2   *The NHS Plan: A plan for investment, a plan for reform* (Cm 4818-I), The Stationery Office, July 2000

3   Wilson T, Roland M, Ham C. The contribution of general practice and the general practitioner to NHS patients. *J R Soc Med* 2006; 99; 24–28

4   Professor Sir Denis Pereira Gray, *A dozen facts about general practice primary care*, St Leonard's Research General Practice, University of Exeter; Emeritus Professor of General Practice

5   Marshall M, Noble J, Davies H, Walshe K, Waterman H, Sheaff R, Elwyn G. *Producing information about general practice services that makes sense to patients and the public*, National Primary Care Research and Development Centre, 2005

6   Hann M, Gravelle H. The maldistribution of general practitioners in England and Wales 1974-2003. *Br J Gen Pract* 2004; 54; 894–8

7   Recent Glasgow University study, plus also Department of Health workforce census figures

8   Bower P, Sheaff RS, Sibbald B, Campbell S, Roland M, Marshall MN et al. Setting standards based on patients' views on access and continuity: secondary analysis of data from the general practice assessment survey. *BMJ* 2003; 236: 258–60

9   Pereira Gray D, Evans P, Sweeney K, Lings P, Seamark D, Seamark C et al. Towards a theory of continuity of care. *J R Soc Medicine* 2003; 96; 160–6

10 Manious A, Baker R, Love M, Pereira Gray DJ, Gill JM. Continuity of care and trust in one's physician: evidence from primary care in the US and UK. *Fam Med* 2001; 33; 22–7

CHAPTER 4

Better access to community services

Better access to community services

This chapter on the wide range of services in the community includes:

- how we will give people more choice and control over their health and care, including extensions of pilots on individual budgets and direct payments;

- expanded use of pharmacies and extended pharmacy services;

- a new urgent care strategy aimed at reducing hospital admissions;

- better access to services which can tackle health, social care, employment and financial needs, including social security benefits;

- improving community services for teenagers, expectant mothers, people with mental health problems, those who have difficulty accessing services, including older people and offenders, and end-of-life care.

Introduction

4.1 Through the *Independence, Well-being and Choice* consultation and *Your health, your care, your say*, people have told us that they want more convenient local health and social care services. In particular, they want different services more closely integrated to meet their needs, with better information provided to the people who use the services. In this chapter, we consider how we can improve the services available in the community when people are ill or need extra support.

4.2 There is, of course, a major difference between the NHS and the social care services provided or funded by local authorities. With the exception of charges for prescriptions and a few other items (which are only free for those on low incomes), NHS care is free at the point of use.

4.3 But social care – in other words, support for the normal activities of our daily lives – is something that we generally provide for ourselves and each other. Indeed, it is a strength of our society and community that we often provide this for our children, family, friends and neighbours.

4.4 Sometimes, however, the needs of individuals go beyond what friends and family can cope with. It is in these situations that we ensure that local services are available and that, through local government, public resources get to those who need the most help and who cannot afford to pay for that extra support themselves.

4.5 Social care is not a universal service. Currently about 1.7 million adults receive social care and support commissioned by local authorities, while many others organise and commission services themselves. Some people are not clear about what their eligibility for local authority-funded care may be in the future, and this could be a source of uncertainty and anxiety.

4.6 From the public's point of view, however, there may seem to be little difference in practice between health and social care services. This extends even further into the benefits system; often a careful assessment of health and care needs provides the information needed to claim social security benefits, such as disability living allowance, attendance allowance and incapacity benefit. Advice on claiming benefits needs to go hand in hand with advice on being able to work and maximise family income. The public is often frustrated by the failure of different services to share information and to integrate services. "Why do I have to tell my story over and over again?" several people asked during the national Citizens' Summit.

4.7 Our goal throughout is to put the public at the centre of the services they receive, and – where services come from different providers, as they often must – to integrate those services as effectively as possible.

4.8 We recognise, of course, that the different funding regimes are a barrier to integrated services. They stem from the decision made by the country in 1948 that, while health services would be paid for and organised nationally, care services would be provided and funded according to local decisions, taken by local people, through local government.

4.9 This devolution of control and power has been a great strength of local government. But without clear national standards it has also led to inequalities in access across the country and sometimes even within neighbouring communities.

4.10 It is clear that people need different kinds of support at different stages of their life. An estimated 30 per cent of adults pay for their own residential care. Other social care services are currently means-tested in most areas, and subject to contributions from those with income and assets that exceed certain thresholds – in accordance with government guidance on 'fairer charging'.[1]

4.11 Local authorities have varying resource levels and must set their own priorities according to local circumstances and needs. Because of this local priority-setting, local authorities may provide differing types and levels of support for different intensities of need, may apply different standards for means testing, and may charge different prices for similar kinds of support.

4.12 This can lead to differences in the services that are available and in the level of access that people may have to those services through the application of Fair Access to Care Services (FACS) criteria. However, local decision-making is also closer to local communities, meaning that local people have opportunities to influence decisions about resources, charging and priorities.

4.13 People have suggested to us that we should look at making charging regimes and eligibility for services more uniform across the country. However, any conclusion about future charging arrangements and the consequences of local decision-making has to be delivered in the context of the wider agenda of local government reform.

4.14 The funding of local services is being considered by Sir Michael Lyons, Professor of Public Policy at the University of Birmingham, as part of his independent inquiry into local government, in which he is examining the future role and function of local government before making recommendations on funding reforms. As part of its analysis, the inquiry is considering some critical issues including fairness, accountability and efficiency, as well as questions about the role of local government in making decisions on local service priorities.

4.15 Sir Michael's final report will inform the 2007 Comprehensive Spending Review. The independent review of social care for older people currently being undertaken for the King's Fund by Sir Derek Wanless – author of the major report on NHS funding published in April 2002 – which is reporting in spring 2006, will also be an important contribution to this discussion.

4.16 Within current funding, however, there is much we can do to further improve health and care services. We set out our proposals below.

Giving people more choice and control over their care services

4.17 There is growing evidence that, where people are actively involved in choosing services and making decisions about the kind of treatment and care they get, the results are better. In addition, as we ask people to take more responsibility for making choices in their lives that will promote their health and independence, we should offer them a greater say in the services we provide.

4.18 In theory, people have always had a choice of GP. In the previous chapter, we explained how we will make that choice more real in practice. About 1.7 million adults receive support and care from services commissioned or directly provided by local authorities, and we will give more of them a greater say in the services they receive.

4.19 Following the direction set out in *Independence, Well-being and Choice*, we will move from a system where

people have to take what is offered to one where people have greater control over identifying the type of support or help they want, and more choice about and influence over the services on offer.

4.20 We plan to do this by giving everyone better information and signposting services better, putting people at the centre of the assessment process, increasing the take-up of direct payments, and introducing individual budgets that will give people greater freedom to select the type of care or support they want.

Direct payments

4.21 Direct payments – cash in lieu of social services – were introduced in 1997. Since 2001, direct payments have also been available to carers, parents of disabled children and 16- and 17-year-olds.

Direct payments have given people real choice and control:

"Direct payments have completely changed my life; choice over who comes into my home equals respect and dignity."

"I have a baby and a direct payment means I can go out when I want. I know who is coming, when they are coming and they know my routine and how I like things done."

4.22 Direct payments are a way for people who need social services to have more control over the service they receive. People who are eligible for services (day care, personal care, respite care, equipment and adaptations) can opt to receive the money for the service from the local authority and purchase it themselves. In this way they can choose the exact service they want, when they want it and who provides it.

4.23 We want more people to enjoy these benefits. Due to the strong response to this issue in *Independence, Well-being and Choice*, we will seek to extend the availability of direct payments to those groups who are excluded under the current legislation.

4.24 Although the take-up of direct payments, for those who are currently eligible, was initially slow, there have been increases in recent years (from 9,000 adults receiving a direct payment in 2002/03 to 24,500 in 2004/05). We expect to see the take-up of direct payments grow much further and faster, as the number of people who currently benefit is only a fraction of the number who could.

CASE STUDY

Client cards for care

Direct payments give people more control, and Kent County Council has come up with an innovative way of allowing people to spend their direct payments easily. They have been trialling a client card, which is designed so that people receiving services can purchase their own care, and works in a very similar way to a normal debit card. People are told how much money is available to them, and they then use the card to spend the money to meet their needs.

The trial has been run with 30 people. Initial findings are that the client card has dramatic potential to reduce transaction costs and is giving people more flexibility in purchasing.

4.25 We have already acted. We have changed the law so that where there was a power, there is now a duty so that councils must make a direct payment to people who can consent to have them. This means that direct payments should be discussed as a first option with everyone, at each assessment and each review.

4.26 In addition, the take-up of direct payments is now an indicator in the Commission for Social Care and Inspection's performance assessment regime, and contributes to the overall star rating of a local authority.

4.27 Beyond this, we expect local authorities to set challenging targets for the take-up of direct payments. In order to help with this we have produced user-friendly information, *A guide to receiving direct payments from your local council*. In association with the Council for Disabled Children, we have also produced *A Parent's Guide to Direct Payments* for parents of disabled children.

4.28 Finally, we will launch a national campaign, working with a range of external stakeholders to increase awareness and improve understanding of the benefits of direct payments.

Individual budgets

4.29 Although direct payments have helped to transform the lives of many people, it can sometimes be difficult for people to make full use of them because of the degree of responsibility involved in managing all aspects of a budget, for example in becoming the employer of a care assistant. For some people, direct payments in cash are likely to remain an attractive option, but for others we want to develop a system that has the advantages without the downsides.

4.30 That is why we announced the development of individual budgets in *Independence, Well-being and Choice*. Individual budgets offer a radical new approach, giving greater control to the individual, opening up the range and availability of services to match needs, and stimulating the market to respond

to new demands from more powerful users of social care.

4.31 Direct payments only cover local authority social care budgets, but individual budgets will bring together separate funds from a variety of agencies including local authority social services, community equipment, Access to Work, independent living funds, disabled facilities grants and the Supporting People programme.

4.32 Individuals who are eligible for these funds will then have a single transparent sum allocated to them in their name and held on their behalf, rather like a bank account. They can choose to take this money out either in the form of a direct payment in cash, as provision of services, or as a mixture of both cash and services, up to the value of their total budget. This will offer the individual much more flexibility to choose services which are more tailored to their specific needs.

4.33 The Department of Health is fully committed to working with the Department for Work and Pensions and the Office of the Deputy Prime Minister to pilot individual budgets for older and disabled people. The first pilot in West Sussex began at the end of 2005, and 12 more will be underway during the first part of 2006. These pilots will run for between 18 months and two years and, if successful, will form the spearhead of a national implementation that could begin as early as 2009/10.

Individual budgets – how they might operate

Mike is 24 years old, and was a sporty and active member of his community until a motorbike accident last year left him paralysed from the waist down. While in hospital he has been worrying about everything he will have to do to get his life back in order, for example the different agencies he will have to contact and the number of assessments he might have to undergo.

Now he is well into his programme of rehabilitation, however, he is keen to use his individual budget to get back to leading his everyday life. His employers have been sympathetic, and Access to Work[2] will be able to support him back into employment. He was already living in a ground-floor flat, but that will need a ramp adaptation to help him get in and out easily. Although he has made really good progress and has regained mobility with his new

wheelchair, he is always going to need some help to get up in the morning, so it looks like a personal assistant would be a good idea.

Mike knows what he is entitled to and knows he has support to get the right services. He really appreciates the support he has access to, including from another wheelchair user of his own age who can talk to him about getting back to work after their experience. This support comes from the local Centre for Independent Living, which is working with the council to help people in their area to manage their individual budgets.

Of course, getting these different streams of support was always possible under the old system but it's so much easier now for someone like Mike to feel secure, knowing what resources are available to him, and that he has help to work out how to use them.

4.34 In addition, we will invite all local authorities to join a support network to help them implement approaches to putting people in control of the services they use. The network will share emerging findings from the pilot programme, and will try out and accelerate the implementation of best practice approaches to self-directed care.

4.35 Furthermore, we will explore the potential for including transport in some of the individual budget pilots, and for the expansion of the individual budget concept further to take on a wider range of income streams, taking into account the progress made on the pilots. We will ask the support network to report on this to the Prime Minister in the summer of 2007. More broadly, we will also ensure that we join up the developmental work on individual budgets and the continuing development of the welfare reform programme.

4.36 The individual budgets pilot programme is currently restricted to adults. However, the Department for Education and Skills, working closely with the Department of Health, is looking at the potential for further pilots, including disabled children. This scoping work is expected to be completed in the summer of 2006.

4.37 This new approach will require radical changes to the way services are organised and delivered. Giving people an individual budget will stimulate the social care market to provide the services people actually want and will help shift resources away from services that do not meet needs or expectations.

4.38 It will also provide greater opportunities for people using services to control the quality of what is on offer and for providers to develop new and more flexible service models, which meet needs in, for example, a more culturally sensitive way or in a more appropriate location for a rural population.

4.39 It has been suggested that we should extend the principle of individual budgets and direct payments to the NHS. We do not propose to do so, since we believe this would compromise the founding principle of the NHS that care should be free at the point of need. Social care operates on

a different basis and has always included means testing and the principles of self and co-payment for services.

Risk management

4.40 *Independence, Well-being and Choice* encouraged a debate about risk management, and consulted on the right balance between protecting individuals and enabling them to make their own decisions about their lives, including assessment of the risks that such decisions might involve.

4.41 There were concerns that some of the proposals, principally those relating to direct payments and individual budgets, might expose people in some situations to unmanageable levels of risk via a potentially unregulated and under-trained workforce. Many respondents called for a national approach to risk management to address these issues for social care.

4.42 There is currently a multitude of guidelines available to health and social care professionals in multi-disciplinary settings. There is now a need for standardised procedures for identification of risk and appropriate responses among team members. **We therefore propose, working closely with other government departments and stakeholders, to develop a national approach to risk management in social care to address these issues over the coming year.**

Somerset STARS nurses help keep people independent at home

Sister Brenda Tompkins has been part of STARS (Short-Term Re-ablement Service) since it was set up by South Somerset PCT in October 2004. This innovative at-home nursing team, run by the PCT, covers a radius of nine miles from South Petherton Hospital and provides care for seven days or more after leaving hospital, allowing people to return to their own homes and regain their independence.

"You get into people's homes and see all sorts of things that need doing – if they need a new piece of equipment, for instance, or we may suggest they start going to a day centre. We work very closely with district nurses, social workers or even the fire safety people. The ambulance team might ring us and ask us to check on people over the weekend. We also do night sits for people who are on a 48-hour trial home from hospital and who aren't sure if they're safe to be at home. We're very flexible.

"There's a big difference for patients from being in hospital, to being on your own. How do you carry a cup of tea when you're walking with a frame? Working out the right pills to take can be quite hard if you have to do it on your own. We want people to be able to stay in their own homes if that's what they want.

"Palliative care is part of our remit and of course we do night or afternoon sits so that the carer can go out for a while or just have a rest. Terminally ill patients have priority, especially if they want to die at home.

"It's been a total eye-opener for me and the staff who work with us and of course we really enjoy this type of nursing, going out into the community."

Community health services

4.43 Most Primary Care Trusts (PCTs) directly provide community health services themselves. PCTs employ about 250,000 staff directly, including district and community nurses, community midwives, health visitors, speech and language therapists and physiotherapists.

4.44 There are lots of good examples of the responsive and innovative new services that are being developed by PCTs. Increasingly, primary care community services are being developed that work closely with other primary and secondary care services to improve services and integration. Some are being co-located with other community services, others are working virtually and collaboratively. This White Paper aims to further encourage innovative services that respond to the needs of communities. Chapter 7 deals further with PCT provision.

Making better use of community pharmacy services

4.45 Some 94 per cent of the population visits a pharmacy at least once a year and over 600 million prescription items are dispensed annually. The public told us in the *Your health, your care, your say* listening exercise that they want pharmacists to have an increased role in providing support, information and care. Community pharmacies are well placed

to be a first point of call for minor ailments.

4.46 Pharmacies are now offering more services than ever before thanks to the new community pharmacy contract that was introduced in April 2005:

*   Repeat dispensing, for example, means that patients can receive up to a year's supply of medicines without having to revisit their GP each time they need more medicine.
*   Some pharmacists are running dedicated clinics in the pharmacy, for example for people with diabetes, those with high blood pressure or high cholesterol.
*   Signposting people to other health and social care services and to support services, and supporting self care and people's well-being, are now essential services to be provided by every community pharmacy.
*   Many pharmacies are adding consultation areas to provide one-to-one services for patients.

Pharmacy-based anti-coagulant monitoring gives instant results

In Durham, pharmacies are already offering innovative new services.

Anita Burdon is a pharmacist at Lanchester Pharmacy in County Durham, one of three pharmacies and a GP practice in the area which offer anti-coagulant monitoring. "Our patients are normally referred from their GP. We have an initial meeting and thereafter they make appointments with me. I have one patient who's a policeman and works unusual shifts and he'll sometimes pop in during a lunchtime, which I don't mind doing. We work around his shifts. As well as my clinic, I also visit GP surgeries and do home visits for patients who can't get to us. In the past, these people would either have been taken by ambulance to the hospital, or the district nurse would have had to come to their home to take samples."

One of the patients benefiting from the Lanchester service is Frank Redfearn, retired MD of an engineering company, who began using Warfarin in early 1999. "I originally received my treatment at the local hospital and then it involved taking a whole morning off work. Sometimes I'd have to go every week which was very inconvenient because there was only one clinic a week and everyone in the area who was on Warfarin descended on it, so the queues were virtually out of the door!

"I started using the local pharmacy clinic about a year ago. It's pretty efficient and I know all the people who work there. Also, I can walk there; I can't drive any more so if I was still going to the hospital clinic it would mean taking the bus – and there's only one an hour from where we live. The other good thing about the pharmacy is you get the results and the information about whether you need to change the dose straight away. The time is very flexible, too. I just ring and let them know what time I want to be there. I think it's an excellent service and I'm very happy with it."

As Anita says, making things easier for the patient could improve compliance. "There were probably some patients who got tired of going to the hospital for the monitoring because it was so inconvenient and decided not to take their Warfarin any more."

4.47 We will continue to develop the contractual arrangements for community pharmacy services in line with the ambitions set out in this White Paper.

Improving urgent access

4.48 We are already giving people a wider range of services that can provide urgent care. As well as getting an appointment on the same day with their health care practice or going to a hospital accident and emergency (A&E) department, people can now use:

- NHS Direct, which offers advice on self-care and is available 24 hours a day, 365 days a year, via the telephone, internet or interactive TV;
- an NHS Walk-in Centre, usually open from 7am to 10pm weekdays and 9am to 10pm at weekends for mainstream centres, and 7am to 7pm weekdays for centres in commuter areas. There are 71 already open including 2 independent sector operators, with 18 more planned to go live during 2006;
- a minor injuries unit;
- a local pharmacist;
- the local out-of-hours primary care services;
- ambulance services where the care is provided at the scene by a paramedic or emergency care practitioner, or in community social services where these are needed urgently;
- crisis resolution teams (for mental health users);
- support for carers (see Chapter 5).

4.49 Of course, many emergencies require the patient to be taken immediately to hospital. But up to 50 per cent of patients who are now taken to A&E by ambulance could be cared for at the scene or in the community. An even higher proportion of those people who take themselves to A&E could be dealt with, just as well or better, elsewhere.

CASE STUDY

Helping people with diabetes to have more control

Pharmacies in Hillingdon offer services to help people with diabetes manage their condition and improve their overall health, as part of the PCT's Community Pharmacy Diabetes Health Improvement Programme.

John Ferguson, who has had diabetes for 15 years, started visiting his pharmacy for treatment last year.

"Obviously, it's much quicker to go to the pharmacy because it gives you the readout instantly; the pharmacist also advises me on my weight and diet. It's like having a medical check-up every time I visit, and I'm very pleased with that."

John gets his checks from Sharman's Chemist in Northwood where Rikin Patel practises:

"In the pharmacy, we have the chance to discuss the medication, explain how it works, when it should be taken, and why it may be changed. Our appointments last between 45 minutes and an hour, so we have time to educate the patients to help themselves as well as doing the tests on the spot and giving people their results. We explain how the medicines work, because if people understand their medication, they're more likely to take it. I think, because of this service, people use their treatments to their best advantage."

Urgent care: to put patients first

The urgent care strategy will focus on improving patient experience and significantly reducing unnecessary admissions to hospitals by:

- introducing simpler ways to access care and ensuring that patients are assessed and directed, first time, to the right service for treatment or help;

- building upon best practice to develop the next phase of quality, cost-effective, primary care out-of-hours services;

- ensuring that the quality of care is consistent for patients across the country, whether care is provided over the telephone, in patients' homes or in a fixed location such as a Walk-in Centre, health centre or A&E;

- encouraging all health partners to work together in a system-wide approach to developing urgent care services that is consistent with other priorities set out in this White Paper, including better care for patients with long-term conditions, shifting care from acute hospitals to the community, promoting better public health, integration with social care and improving access to GPs in-hours;

- improving joint PCT and local authority commissioning arrangements to ensure better integration across services, make the best use of resources and prevent duplication. This will be particularly important for telephone and telecare services, and those provided in the patient's home;

- providing high-quality mobile health care for patients who need urgent care, through implementation of *Taking healthcare to the patient*. Over the next five years, ambulance trusts will increasingly work as part of the primary care team to help provide diagnostic services and to support patients with long-term conditions. They will continue to improve the speed and quality of ambulance responses to 999 calls;

- developing a multi-disciplinary workforce strategy that makes the best use of local skills and expertise, and supports the training and educational needs of staff providing urgent care to patients;

- ensuring that the IT requirements to deliver urgent care services are reflected in the wider IT agenda;

- ensuring that the skills and experience of NHS Direct are fully utilised by patients and health care organisations. In particular, we would expect NHS Direct to play a key role in enabling patients to self care where this is appropriate. NHS Direct could also help to provide better information about local services;

- providing guidance and advice, sharing learning and best practice examples, and providing toolkits to support health and social care economies to develop integrated urgent care services that meet the needs of patients locally.

4.50 The present system of urgent and emergency care can be extremely frustrating for patients, with delays and duplication, and patients being handed over from one service to another. Out-of-hours patients may have to repeat their details as many as four times in a disjointed journey to definitive care. Nor does the system get the best value for NHS resources.

4.51 During 2006 we will develop an urgent care service strategy for the NHS, providing a framework within which PCTs and local authorities can work (see box). This will take full account of the implications for other providers, including social care and ambulance services.

4.52 A number of changes are being made to the Payment by Results tariff to create appropriate financial incentives and financial stability to better support delivery of urgent care in the NHS. As set out in the recent publication on the rules for the NHS in 2006/07:
- In the longer term we will develop a single tariff that applies to similar attendances in A&E, minor injuries units and Walk-in Centres, so that funding is governed by the type of treatment and not where it is delivered. As a first step, in 2006//07 there will be one tariff for minor attendances at A&E and attendance at minor injuries units.

- A reduced rate tariff will apply to emergency admissions above and below a threshold. This will help manage the overall level of risk of inappropriate growth in emergency admissions and share the financial risk between providers and commissioners.
- The short-stay tariff (which results in a reduction for stays of less than two days for defined Healthcare Resource Groups within tariff) has been revised to more closely align the tariff with the actual cost of short stays.

Rapid access to sexual health services

4.53 Access to sexual health services also needs to be faster. As part of our comprehensive strategy for improving the sexual health of the population, investment in services will mean that we will improve prevention and access to treatment for sexually transmitted infections (STIs), human immunodeficiency virus (HIV) and reproductive health, including conception, and by 2008 everyone will have access to a genito-urinary medicine (GUM) clinic within 48 hours.

4.54 In addition, big increases in demand for sexual health services mean it is no longer sensible or economic to deliver sexual health care, particularly STI management, only in hospital-based specialist services. This is because many sexual health services can now be effectively delivered in a range of settings.

Self-testing on your high street

It is not always easy to get young adults to test themselves for STIs. They do not always use traditional health services, but most will be buying beauty products. So a partnership between Boots and the Department of Health has led to chlamydia screening kits being available in Boots stores across London.

This pilot scheme has been running since November 2005 and is proving popular. It marks a real attempt to bring screening to patients, rather than relying on them seeking a test. Hopefully the result will be an earlier detection of chlamydia to allow more rapid treatment.

Kits are free to people aged between 16 and 24. They return a urine sample which is sent off to a laboratory. They receive the result within three to seven days by a method of their choosing – by text, phone or letter. Text has been the most popular method to date.

Patients who test positive are contacted by Camden Chlamydia Screening Office who give advice on the treatment options available.

Twenty-three-year-old Alice, who tested negative, explains why she used the Boots service. "I was really embarrassed about having a chlamydia test and had put it off for ages because I didn't want to go to my doctor. When I heard Boots were offering testing free I went along. It was really quick and the pharmacist was really helpful. I was really glad I finally got it done."

4.55 To meet the needs and preferences of service users, PCTs should aim to commission a full range of services, which provide different levels of sexual health care in a variety of settings. *Choosing Health*, recommended standards for HIV and sexual health services recommend the development of local managed networks for sexual health, in particular as regards young people. These networks will help to provide a comprehensive service to meet local people's needs.

4.56 The management of STIs should be developed and expanded in community settings and general practice. The voluntary and business sectors can also play a key role as they are in the national chlamydia screening programme and the 'Chlamydia Screening in Boots' pilot. Services can be nurse-led and make full use of nurse prescribing and Patient Group Directions. These arrangements should be overseen by clinical specialists who can provide the back-up to frontline services for people with complex needs.

Rapid access to mental health services

4.57 Rapid access to mental health services is also crucial in times of stress and crisis. Good progress has been made in implementing recommendations from the *National Service Framework for Mental Health* to establish multi-skilled community mental health teams to help people get the right support at the right time, without necessarily having to go into hospital.

4.58 Some of these teams are generic and some have specialist functions: crisis resolution teams, early intervention for first onset psychosis, assertive outreach teams, A&E liaison teams, etc. To work properly, and to continue to improve, all these teams need strong liaison and referral arrangements with each other across other parts of the urgent and primary care systems.

CASE STUDY

Crisis resolution in mental health

Birmingham and Solihull Mental Health Trust has one of the longest established crisis resolution teams covering 150,000 people in the Yardley/Hodge Hill area. The team is multi-disciplinary, including psychiatrists, nurses and social workers, and works intensively supporting people in their own homes who are experiencing a mental health crisis and who might otherwise have to be admitted to hospital. This can involve several visits per day using a range of medical and psychosocial interventions, as well as working very closely with family carers.

Service users and carers have welcomed this support as an alternative to hospital admission and the service has proved particularly beneficial to people from minority ethnic groups. In terms of impact, inpatient bed use in this area dropped by 50 per cent within less than a year of the team commencing in 1996 and admissions have remained at that level.

4.59 For young people, child and adolescent mental health services (CAMHS) provide support. By the end of 2006 there will be access to comprehensive CAMHS across the country – this is a priority and a Public Service Agreement target. However, services need to increase the speed of access to CAMHS so that children and young people are seen more promptly.

4.60 In addition, PCTs have more to do in improving the ways in which CAMHS meet the needs of some groups, most notably children and young people from ethnic minorities, those with learning disabilities, looked-after children and young offenders. Futher work is also required to ensure there is a seamless transfer from CAMHS to adult services.

Screening for cancer

4.61 Screening for cancer is already predominantly a community-based service. Eighty per cent of the 1.3 million mammograms undertaken by the NHS breast screening programme are done in mobile units. The vast majority of the 3.6 million women who attend for cervical screening each year have this done in primary care.

4.62 Both of these screening programmes are highly successful and are contributing to the marked fall in death rates for breast and cervical cancer. The breast screening programme has recently been expanded, resulting in a 31 per cent increase in screen-detected cancers.

Physio by phone

The Physio Direct telephone service was set up by Huntingdonshire PCT following a pilot in 2001. People can ring a dedicated number to speak to a physiotherapist direct.

The physiotherapist is supported by a computer program which records clinical data and assists them in making a diagnosis. The caller receives verbal and written advice on self-management and the physiotherapist sends a report on the outcome of the assessment to the caller's GP, to ensure continuity of care. The physiotherapist may also request a prescription or sickness certificate from the GP without the GP needing to see the patient.

Two-thirds of callers have not needed follow-up after the initial phone call, while other callers have had a subsequent appointment with a physiotherapist. By dealing with many problems over the phone it has reduced demand for GP appointments (30 per cent of GP appointments deal with musculoskeletal problems) and proved convenient for callers.

Robust clinical guidelines ensure the quality of the service and access to specialised services is always available if needed.

4.63 In our election manifesto, we promised to reduce the time taken to get the results of cervical screening back to women. Details of how this will be achieved will be published later this year.

4.64 A new screening programme for bowel cancer will be rolled out from April 2006. This will be one of the first national bowel screening programmes in the world and will be the first cancer screening programme in this country to include men as well as women. When fully operational, around 2 million people each year will be sent a self-sampling kit to use in the privacy of their own homes. The kit is then returned by post to a regional laboratory. A pilot in the West Midlands has run very successfully for several years.

Access to allied health professionals' therapy services

4.65 Self-referral to therapist services has the potential to increase patient satisfaction and save valuable GP time. The *Your health, your care, your say* listening exercise revealed that, while increasing self-referral was not an urgent priority, there was some support for extending this approach. So in order to provide better access to a wider range of services, we will pilot and evaluate self-referral to physiotherapy. We will also consider the potential benefits of offering self-referral for additional direct access for other therapy services.

Nurses near you

Lorraine Elliott from Blackburn North District Nursing Team helped to set up a mobile clinic for men, especially those from ethnic minorities, many of whom don't speak English.

"We wanted to move away from the health centre into other places such as mosques or community centres, where we'd be more likely to reach people. We've been able to give advice, or help them find the right person to go to if they have a particular health problem. The feedback has been very positive."

Asif Hussain, 37, was so impressed with the service provided by the clinic that he encouraged his family and friends to try going there, too.

"I'd only go to the GP if there was something seriously wrong," says Asif. "With the clinic, I walked straight in and had a one-to-one conversation with the health professionals. It was confidential and I could ask questions. They checked my weight, height, BMI (body mass index) and blood sugar, and gave me lifestyle advice. I'd definitely go again."

Reaching out to people in need

4.66 Allowing people to take the lead in accessing the help they need is a fundamental principle we want to uphold, but sometimes health and care services must proactively go out to those who have the greatest needs. This is because some groups, including people who live in residential homes, black and minority ethnic people, people who are homeless or living in temporary accommodation, and travellers, will not always be able to access traditional services, including health care, social services and the benefits system.

4.67 The use of outreach to support these groups is essential if we are going to ensure that equity of access is a reality for people in these groups and if we are to prevent health inequalities increasing. The incentive for PCTs and local authorities to develop outreach services is clear in that it should be cost-effective in tackling conditions early. For instance, early identification of symptoms for care home residents may prevent avoidable hospitalisation.

4.68 The exact nature of the outreach services will depend on the specific needs of the population being served.

4.69 These people can face a range of health problems which can lead to, or be exacerbated by, their housing need. They can also experience difficulty accessing health care.

4.70 The Department of Health and the Office of the Deputy Prime Minister are encouraging housing and health services to work together to improve the well-being of homeless people and to prevent homelessness. They have issued joint guidance[3] on developing shared outcomes for people who are homeless or in temporary accommodation, including improving access to primary health care, improving substance misuse and mental health treatment, and preventing homelessness through appropriate, targeted health support.

4.71 Better partnership working is essential if we are to improve health outcomes and reduce health inequalities for the most vulnerable groups, for instance people who are homeless or living in temporary accommodation.

4.72 For those patients who want to work but their health condition or disability is stopping them from doing so, we are working closely with the Department for Work and Pensions who are piloting offering joint health and employment support in GP surgeries, making it easier for people to access the services they need in a single location.

Expectant mothers

4.73 We want to ensure that maternity services are women-focused and family-centred. This means increasing choice for women and their partners over where and how they have their baby.

CASE STUDY

Nurse practitioner-led outreach services

The Huddersfield Outreach Service, established in December 2002, focuses on the Deighton Ward, which falls into the top 4 per cent most deprived areas in the country. It supports nearly 17,000 families with children, providing immunisation and vaccinations, contraception and advice on sexual health, teenage pregnancy clinics, child health surveillance and help with smoking cessation.

The service operates from four general practices at different sites and uses common clinical systems with a monthly audit to monitor performance. Working with local health visitors, the service offers home visits, same-day services and Monday-to-Friday open access. Childhood immunisations are given, by appointment, in routine general outreach clinics and opportunistically at home. Immunisation coverage of two year olds has steadily increased by around 8 per cent from 79 to 87 per cent. Attendance and access rates have increased and reflect the confidence gained by the local community in the service. The primary care team plan to build on this success and expand the range of services offered by setting themselves up as an alternative personal medical service.

4.74 In *Your health, your care, your say* we heard people praise midwives and the support they provided, but express dissatisfaction that they could not always choose where their baby was born. Increasing choice is not the only priority – surveys of women and their partners have also identified being treated as an individual and being provided with more information as important.

4.75 A truly individualised maternity service will give women as much control as possible during their pregnancy, birth and post-birth. It will mean midwives ensuring that women have all the information they need about this life event. This will include information about the choices available and in formats and styles appropriate to people with different needs, as well as ensuring that they fully understand the financial support available to them and their partner during and after pregnancy. It will mean women can access a midwife directly, without going to their GP first, if that is what they want.

4.76 It will mean a maternity service in which all women are offered a choice of where they have their baby. Wherever possible, this is likely to include offering midwifery-led services provided at home, in a 'home-like' setting or in a hospital, the final choice depending on factors such as individual case needs and geography. Women will also be able to access antenatal and postnatal care in community-based settings, such as Children's Centres.

4.77 It will mean all women will be offered a choice of pain relief appropriate to the setting in which they choose to give birth. It will mean all women having continuity of care before and after birth provided by a midwife they know, and being individually supported throughout the birth. **This will be in place by 2009**.

4.78 To achieve such a world-class maternity service, we commit to three actions. **Firstly, we need to raise the profile of maternity services in both the public and the commissioning agenda. Then we must ensure that Payment by Results supports the choices women make during pregnancy. And finally, we will work with PCTs to review the current maternity workforce and identify where more staff are needed to deliver these commitments.**

4.79 Regrettably, pregnant women are at an increased risk of domestic violence, with 30 per cent of cases starting during pregnancy. To help

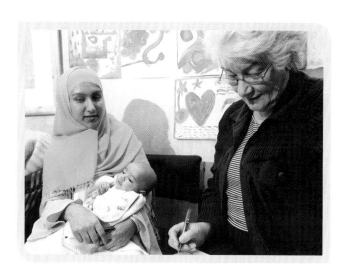

midwives and other health professionals identify and give appropriate support to women who are being abused, we have recently published *Responding to domestic abuse: A handbook for health professionals.*[4]

4.80 This will help the identification of domestic violence as it arises and, where necessary, health professionals should work with social workers and the police and local housing authorities to protect and support the victims of abuse. This is particularly important in safeguarding children in these situations. The potential benefits are huge – not just in terms of reduced harm to the one in four women and one in six men who suffer from domestic violence in their lifetime, but also in reducing the £23 billion domestic violence costs the economy.

Improving immunisation services

4.81 Immunisation remains one of the most effective ways for people to protect themselves or their children against diseases that can kill or cause serious long-term ill-health. Nationally, high levels of immunisation have resulted in a significant reduction in the rate of infectious diseases. However, the current trend of greater numbers of general practices opting out of immunisation service provision in deprived areas[5] means that immunisation services could fail those who need them most, including disadvantaged children, older people, people who move frequently and adults not vaccinated as children – increasing

the likelihood of outbreaks. Alternative models of providing immunisation services are needed to ensure high immunisation coverage for all.

4.82 We know barriers to access exist among disadvantaged groups and we want a wider network of providers and partnerships with GPs, including out-of-hours providers, Walk-in Centres, Children's Centres and outreach services. The full range of primary medical care contracts can be used flexibly depending on local immunisation commissioning priorities, and should help to improve services and the way they are delivered. A principle underlying this change will be that the money spent on immunisation target payments will remain as a whole but is shared across different types of contract. **We are seeking to support the introduction of these changes and will work with NHS Connecting for Health to improve the existing national population-based immunisation reporting system.**

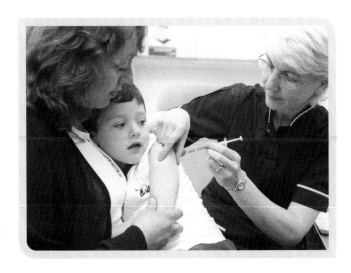

Schooled in health

Following the reorganisation and merger of the previously separate Valley Road Infant and Junior schools in 2002, a new state-of-the-art building was created in Sunderland. The governors used this as an opportunity to make Valley Road Community Primary School the hub of the community. It provides a 'one-stop shop' for health, childcare and social services as well as education for the community.

The school has three wings, two for traditional school use and one for the community. The community wing has a healthy living centre, a neighbourhood nursery providing care for children aged three months to three years all year round, provision for an early years behaviour team and a child and adolescent mental health services team.

The school is committed to developing its services further and to building on the success of the multi-agency working. They want to set up a branch of the local credit union, as well as creating a community art gallery. They also want to landscape the site and make a woodland walkway and community garden.

Ofsted's view is that the project as a whole is bringing hope and optimism to an area of social and economic difficulty, and is impacting on the regeneration of the area. As such it can be viewed as a blueprint for the future. A pupil at the school is more succinct, simply saying "The whole school is brilliant."

4.83 In addition, an immunisation and vaccination commissioning strategy at PCT level is needed. **We will require the Health Protection Agency to develop a new plan for providing immunisation coverage information at postcode to help PCTs monitor pockets of low uptake and to support their commissioning decisions.**

Teenagers

4.84 Teenagers are one group who do not always use traditional NHS services. We have sought to make such services more young people friendly by publishing the *You're Welcome* quality criteria.[6] These criteria reflect the standards set out in the *National Service Framework for Children, Young People and Maternity Services*. An accompanying resource pack, including case studies, helps PCTs and local authorities to develop services that are accessible and trusted by young people.

4.85 We will also be seeking to make health an integral part of the everyday services that young people use. Partly this will be building on the Government's commitment in the *Every Child Matters: Change for Children* programme to develop extended schools so that we provide welcoming and accessible health care in school settings.

4.86 We also expect provision to be made in non-formal educational settings, such as youth centres. The *Youth Matters* Green Paper committed the Government to explore the potential of such settings in 2006 in three adolescent health demonstration sites. We will consider how these sites can be linked to the NHS 'Life Check' at the transition from primary to secondary education.

4.87 Young people's involvement in the design and delivery of these services is fundamental to their success and acceptability. We will start this involvement immediately by working with younger people to ensure that services, such as sexual health, are provided in a way and a location that encourage usage. In addition, making real progress in providing health services in educational and youth-centred settings will require close partnership working between the NHS and local authorities.

People with learning disabilities

4.88 People with learning disabilities face particular health inequalities. The NHS has historically not served such people well and the Department of Health has previously committed to introduce regular, comprehensive health checks for learning disabled people. These would help to direct people into the system, from which point onwards they will be better positioned to receive good quality health care. **We will review the best way to deliver on this earlier commitment.**

4.89 People with learning disabilities also want greater choice and control over their own lives, in line with the principles of the *Valuing People*[7] White Paper.

4.90 This includes being supported to live in ordinary housing in their local community and to work. Even today, close to 3,000 people with learning disabilities live as inpatients in NHS residential accommodation, or 'NHS campuses'. We finally want to see an end to this type of institutional provision. Campus settings limit choices and give poorer outcomes, whereas community-based settings enable a greater degree of independence and inclusion. Campus accommodation also often neglects people's health needs. For example, some campus occupants are being denied their right to register with a GP practice.

Joseph *In Control* thanks to new ways of funding services

Seventeen-year-old Joseph Tomlinson from Wigan has a severe learning disability. Joseph has the same aspirations as any other 17-year-old but faced barriers in achieving them. Now thanks to In Control, a new scheme being pioneered in Wigan, funded by social services, the local education authority, the Learning Skills Council and Independent Living Funds, Joseph can attend the local college, go to the gym and live an ordinary life. His mum Caroline explains how In Control has revolutionised Joseph's life.

"Before the pilot started Joseph went to a special school, a good hour away, and had lots of different carers and found that lack of continuity really difficult. At one point I had 46 different people coming through the house! It was also extremely expensive and Joseph really wasn't receiving the benefit. We were totally dependent on whatever support was prescribed for him. In Control means people who need support are given both the money and the freedom to choose and buy the services they need, so it has enabled us to choose the services that Joseph needs.

"We decided that Joseph needed to be able to do the same things as other young people of his age and that it was very important for him to have continuity of care, so that the same people stayed with him.

"Although we could have used an agency, we decided to employ a team of personal assistants to support him directly. There are six of them altogether and the assistants support him throughout the day inside and outside college, during the week and at the weekend. It has raised the quality of his life phenomenally – before this scheme started he wouldn't have been able to do three-quarters of the things he does now, like go away for the weekend or go to the gym. If we do something as a family he can come with one of his supporters. He is so much happier. Most importantly he has continuity in the people who work with him, they are people he has chosen to be with."

4.91 There is a strong evidence base to support moving all people with learning disabilities from campus accommodation and placing them in more community-based settings.[8] However, further consultation on the detailed arrangements is needed so that no individual is moved from a campus until suitable alternative arrangements have been put in place. This will be led by the Valuing People Support Team with a view to ensuring local commissioners achieve the closure of all NHS residential campuses by the end of the decade.

Access to health services for offenders

4.92 Among offenders,[9] there are high levels of need. For instance, 90 per cent of all people entering prison have some form of mental health, personality disorder or substance misuse problem. Many will therefore be unemployed, and having been in prison forms an extra barrier to finding work when they are discharged.

4.93 There is also a high incidence of mental health problems among young offenders, many of whom have been in local authority care, have suffered violence at home and have reported sexual abuse.

4.94 PCTs already have responsibility for commissioning services for offenders in the community. From April 2006 (although some are already doing so), all PCTs will also have responsibility for commissioning services for prisons within their geographical area and all health services for young people in young offender institutions and secure training centres.

4.95 Those who offend often have a significant profile of other needs, including health needs. Many who find themselves in contact with the criminal justice system have drug, alcohol or mental health (or a combination of these) problems. Whether in a community or prison setting, PCTs have an excellent opportunity to work with offenders to tackle these issues, with considerable potential gains for society and health services. Joint work between the health and criminal justice systems offers real potential to reduce health inequalities **and** crime, as does integrated working between health, education, social care and youth justice in youth offending teams.

4.96 PCTs should be working with probation services and local authorities to meet the needs of offenders. During the *Your health, you care, your say* consultation, offenders voiced the opinion that public services were hard to access and that there was little support with finding housing, jobs or health services.

4.97 Local health and criminal justice commissioners should ensure that health and social care interventions are accessible to offenders, especially aspects like crisis intervention or ongoing community psychiatric nurse support. This might also mean services are co-located or provided in places where offenders go to receive their community supervision.

Older people

4.98 In the *Independence, Well-being and Choice* and *Your health, your care, your say* consultations people expressed concern about meeting the needs of older people, particularly those with dementia.

4.99 The National Clinical Director for Older People will shortly be publishing plans for improving services for older people in a *Next Steps* document covering three themes: dignity in care, responsive services and active ageing. This will include detailed plans for ensuring dignity in all care settings and at the end of life, improved services for people with strokes, falls, dementia, multiple conditions and complex needs, and information technology for personalised care and for promoting healthy active life, independence, well-being and choice for older people.

4.100 We have already set out plans for improving services for older people with mental health problems, including dementia, in *Everybody's Business – Integrated mental health services for older adults: a service development guide.*[10] Commissioners and providers of services will need to become familiar with this guide as it provides the blueprint for meeting the needs of dementia sufferers close to home.

End-of-life care

4.101 Over 500,000 adults die in England each year. Although over 50 per cent of people say they would like to be cared for and die at home if they were terminally ill, at present only 20 per cent of people die at home.[11] In the *Your health, your care, your say* consultation people told us that they wanted the choice to die at home, although they also recognised that this might be difficult for the dying person's family, who would also need support.

4.102 The Government recognises that additional investment is needed to improve end-of-life care and has pledged to increase choices for patients by doubling investment in palliative care services. This will give more people the choice to be treated at home when they are dying, but we must also recognise the wishes of any family members who are caring for dying relatives.

4.103 To allow this choice, we will establish end-of-life care networks, building on the co-operative approach suggested by the new urgent care strategy (see paragraph 4.51 above). These will improve service co-ordination and help identify all patients in need. The networks will bring together primary care services, social services, hospices and third-sector providers, community-based palliative care services, as well as hospital services. This approach will build on pilots being undertaken with Marie Curie Cancer

Care through the Delivering Choice Programme sites.

4.104 We will ensure all staff who work with people who are dying are properly trained to look after dying patients and their carers. This will mean extending the roll-out of tools such as the Gold Standard Framework and the Liverpool Care Pathway for the Dying to cover the whole country.

4.105 We will build on co-ordinated multi-agency assessments, ensuring health, education and social care services are organised around the needs of the dying person and his or her family.

4.106 We will provide rapid response (hospice at home) services to patients in need by investing in community-based specialist palliative care services. Further details will be provided in due course on the distribution of funding to meet these commitments.

4.107 For disabled children, children with complex health needs and those in need of palliative care, PCTs should ensure that the right model of service is developed by undertaking a review to audit capacity (including children's community nursing) and delivery of integrated care pathways against National Service Framework standards, agreeing service models, funding and commissioning arrangements with their SHAs.

4.108 Support for carers when the cared-for person is dying is especially important and this will be taken into account in developing the New Deal for Carers described in the next chapter.

4.109 There are those that need to receive care from more than one primary care community service. And, as the population ages, the number of people with ongoing needs that will affect their daily lives will increase. We must confront this challenge. Otherwise people will receive poorly co-ordinated care that is unnecessarily expensive.

References

1   *Fairer charging policies for home care and other non-residential social services – a consultation document and draft guidance*, Department of Health, 2001

2   Access to Work is run by Jobcentre Plus. See this link: www.jobcentreplus.gov.uk/ JCP/Customers/HelpForDisabledPeople/ AccesstoWork/

3   *Achieving positive shared outcomes in health and homelessness*, Department of Health and Office of the Deputy Prime Minister, March 2004

4   *Responding to domestic abuse: A handbook for health professionals*, Department of Health, 2006

5   12.5% of general practices in the most deprived fifth of PCTs have opted out, compared with only 0.2% in the least deprived fifth. (Department of Health, 2005, unpublished)

6   *You're welcome quality criteria: Making health services young people friendly*, October 18, 2005

7   *Valuing People: A new strategy for Learning Disability for the 21st Century*, March 20, 2001

8   Emerson et al, 1999, *Quality and costs of residential supports for people with learning disabilities: A comparative analysis of quality and costs in village communities, residential campuses and dispersed housing schemes, summary and implications*

9   The term 'offender' is taken here in its widest context to include not only those charged or sentenced within the criminal justice system, which will include those in prisons and under supervision of the probation service, but also those known to commit offences by the police

10   *Everybody's Business-Integrated mental health services for older adults: a service development guide*, Community Services Improvement Partnership, November 2005

11   Higginson, I. (2003) *Priorities and Preferences for End of Life Care*, NCHSPCS, 2003

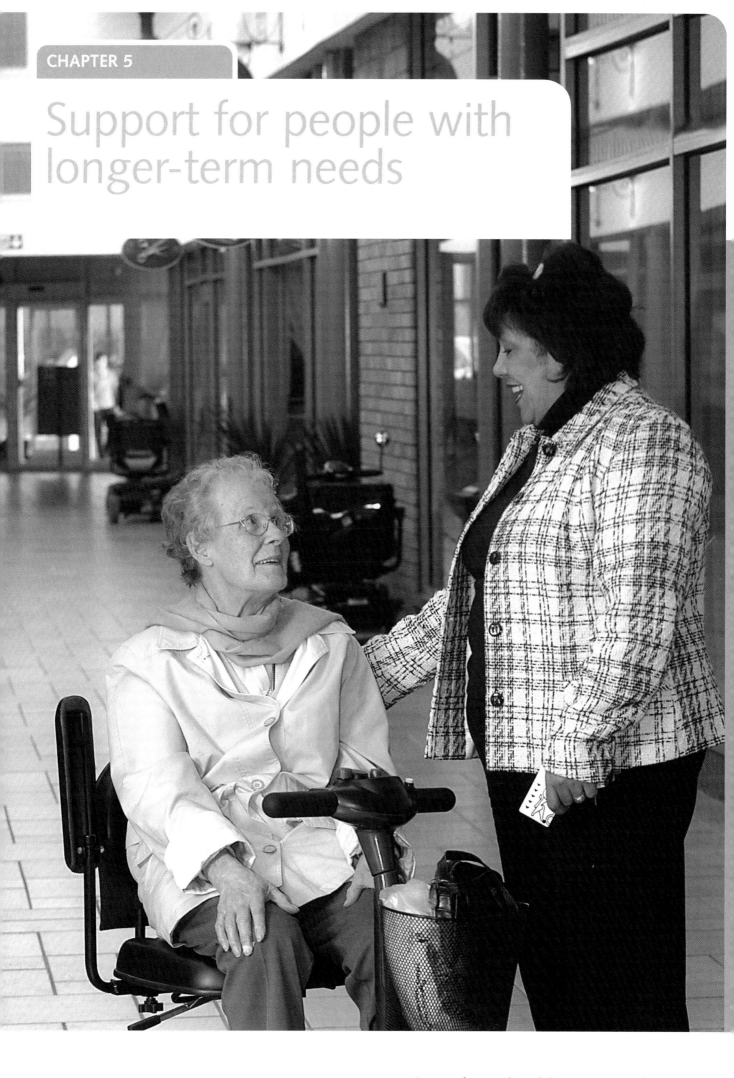

CHAPTER 5

Support for people with longer-term needs

Support for people with longer-term needs

This chapter on ongoing care and support includes discussion of:

- empowering those with long-term needs to do more to care for themselves, including better access to information and care plans;
- investment in training and development of skills for staff who care for people with ongoing needs;
- new supports for informal carers including a helpline, short-term respite and training;
- collaboration between health and social care to create multi-disciplinary networks to support those people with the most complex needs.

Introduction

5.1 People with longer-term or more complex health and social care needs want services that will help them to maintain their independence and well-being and to lead as fulfilling a life as possible.

5.2 *Independence, Well-being and Choice* set out a vision and aims for adult social care and wider services and these have been warmly welcomed by the public and stakeholders. This is the vision that we are adopting and which we will support towards implementation.

5.3 Participants in the *Your health, your care, your say* consultation told us that they have seen significant improvement in services. People with asthma, diabetes, heart disease and cancer said that services had improved substantially and praised the specially trained staff and specific clinics that were now in place.

5.4 The wider use of a range of evidence-based good practice, including the National Service Frameworks for most of the common long-term conditions[1] and the NHS and social care long-term conditions model,[2] have helped to bring about these improvements. Key elements of best clinical practice for some conditions are also now embedded in the Quality and Outcomes Framework (QOF) for GPs (see Chapter 2). In addition, the Social Care Institute for Excellence (SCIE) has been working

with people and organisations throughout the social care sector to identify useful information, research and examples of good practice.

5.5 In spite of this, people remain concerned about poor co-ordination between health and social care services, and want more support for independent living. Overall, the current interface between health and social care appears confusing, lacking in co-ordination and can feel fragmented to the individual. There are also still too many people in need of emergency care because their day-to-day care has broken down. In too many cases, this is distressing and would not be necessary if care were better maintained. For many people barriers to the use of universal services create problems in daily life.

The strategic challenge

5.6 There are over 15 million people in England with longer-term health needs. They are a large and growing group. We estimate that every decade, from ageing of the population alone, the number of people with long-term conditions will increase by over a million. The number of people aged 85 years and over is projected to rise by nearly 75 per cent by 2025. The number of people with severe disability will also increase as prevalence rises among children, partly due to the increased survival of pre-term babies.

5.7 Over two-thirds of NHS activity relates to the one-third of the population with the highest needs of these kinds, and an estimated 80 per cent of costs.[3] This will have significant resource implications both for health and social care, unless we change our current approach.

5.8 Recent national surveys show that we still need to do more to empower people with long-term health and social care needs through greater choice and more control over their care. Over a third of those receiving social care had not had a review in the last year. Half of all people with long-term conditions were not aware of treatment options and did not have a

clear plan that lays out what they can do for themselves to manage their condition better. As a consequence a significant proportion of all medicines are not taken as intended.

5.9 Health and care services still do not focus sufficiently on supporting people to understand and take control at an early stage of their condition. As a result, resources are wasted, medication goes unused, people's health deteriorates more quickly than it should and quality of life is compromised.

Figure 5.1 Responses from people with long-term conditions
Services that could be made available – which are relevant to you and which would you use?

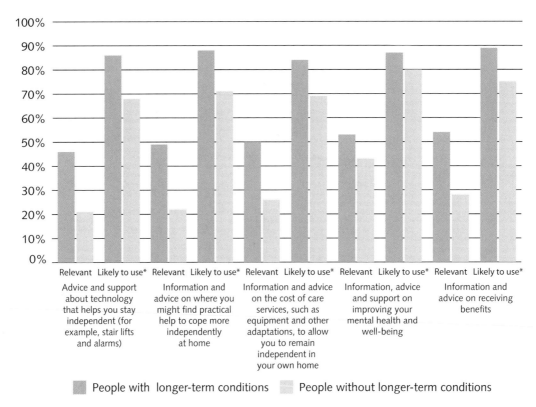

People with longer-term conditions   People without longer-term conditions

Source: *Your health, your care, your say* questionnaire
N = 25,666 then weighted for population
* Total out of those who said it was relevant

5.10 The four central aims of this White Paper – derived as they are from people's responses to our consultation – have special force and relevance to those with longer-term problems:

- better health and well-being;
- convenient access to high-quality services;
- support for those in greatest need;
- care in the most appropriate setting, closer to home.

These concepts come together in looking at how to improve care for this group. As a result of this group's higher level of need, they also had higher interest and perceived value from potential additional services.

5.11 Our aim for people with longer-term needs is the same as our aim for all people who use services. Services should support people to take greater control over their own lives and should allow everyone to enjoy a good quality of life, so that they are able to contribute fully to our communities. They should be seamless, proactive and tailored to individual needs. There needs to be a greater focus on prevention and the early use of low-level support services, such as those provided through the Supporting People programme.

5.12 People need to be treated sooner, nearer to home and before their condition causes more serious problems. Individuals need information, signposting and support, so that they

Fig 5.2 Empowering and enabling individuals to take control

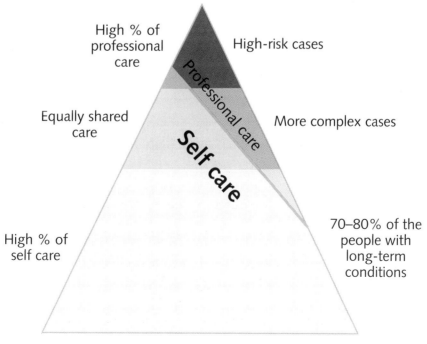

High % of professional care

High-risk cases

Professional care

Equally shared care

More complex cases

Self care

High % of self care

70–80% of the people with long-term conditions

Source: Department of Health

can take control and make informed choices about their care and treatment. Wherever possible, they should be enabled to use the wide range of services available to the whole community, for example housing, transport and leisure.

5.13 We need to move from fragmented to integrated service provision, from an episodic focus to one of continuing relationships – relationships that are flexible enough to respond to changing needs. Long-term conditions do not mean a steady decline in well-being. People's needs may fluctuate markedly and health and social care must be able to respond to these.

5.14 We will empower people to take more control of the management of their needs and take steps to ensure that people with ongoing needs are assessed more quickly and effectively. Finally, we will ensure there are effective programmes of support available, including for people who care for others.

Helping people take control

Supporting self care
5.15 People will be supported to take better control of their care and condition through a wide range of initiatives. These include a major new focus on self care and self-management. We will also provide additional support to carers.

5.16 A comprehensive framework with guidelines on developing local strategies to support self care for people with long-term conditions will be published by the Department of Health shortly after this White Paper. The following initiatives will strengthen this integrated approach.

Helping individuals manage their own care better
5.17 The Expert Patients Programme (EPP) provides training for people with a chronic condition to develop the skills they need to take effective control of their lives. Training is led by people who have personal experience of living with a long-term illness. We will increase EPP capacity from 12,000 course places a year to over 100,000 by 2012. The EPP course needs to be able to diversify and respond better to the needs of its participants. The EPP also needs a sustainable financial future in the context of a developing market place and Practice Based Commissioning (PBC).

5.18 To achieve this, and create security and continuity for supported self-management, a community interest

Peer advisers giving more control to people

By becoming experts in their own health condition, people can improve the quality of their own life and help others. Weston Area Health Trust and North Somerset Primary Care Trust (PCT) have recognised this and have established a peer adviser group for diabetes.

Peer advisers are given training and then pass their expertise on to others. Patients and carers relate well to peer advisers as they have been in the same situation. In North Somerset, peer advisers have also become trainers on self care courses and their knowledge has meant they have made effective suggestions in improving care.

One of the people on the peer adviser training programme commented, "I would like to help prevent the long-term complications that can be avoided by a change of lifestyle now and hopefully help others to do the same. From a personal point of view, I couldn't have asked for a better opportunity than this, which I have been privileged to take part in."

Staff involved in the peer advisers programme said: "Attending the sessions as a facilitator has given me an in-depth insight into the disease and the patients' concerns. This is transferable to my job. My lasting thought is that they are 'people with diabetes' and not just 'diabetic patients' and that the patient wants to lead a normal life. Through this programme we can support them."

In the future there are plans to extend the peer adviser model to other ongoing conditions. Peer advisers will also be involved in PBC as it develops in North Somerset, to ensure services develop to meet people's needs.

company will be established to market and deliver self-management courses. Courses will be designed to meet people's different needs, including those in marginalised groups. Health and social care organisations can then commission courses from this new provider.

5.19 The new community interest company will provide the opportunity to develop new courses, make its products available in new markets and develop new partnerships with all stakeholders involved in self care support.

5.20 So we plan to treble investment in the EPP and support its transition to a social enterprise organisation.

5.21 Alongside the specific EPP programme, our health reform drivers will also encourage primary care providers and others to focus their efforts more strongly on promoting individuals' abilities to manage their own conditions better. Individual budgets in social care have this personal empowerment at their heart. Our proposals to strengthen patient choice of primary care practices will do the same. Practices that offer support to expert patient groups and other ways of empowering self care will attract more registrations, gain resources and develop specialist expertise.

5.22 Finally, we will get a much stronger focus on improving self care through both the QOF and the standards published by the Department of Health.

Engaging general practice in self care

5.23 One of the main ways these initiatives can be brought together and delivered is through general practice, building on their responsibility for co-ordination of care. The new focus on health and well-being outcomes in the QOF will help. We need to go further. We will seek to ensure that practices use the information in their QOF registers to effectively commission services that

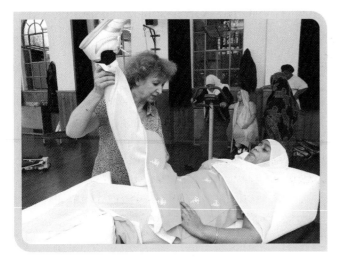

support self care for patients with long-term conditions and ask NHS Employers to consider the involvement of general practice in promoting self care as one of the highest priorities for future changes to contractual arrangements.

Improved health and social care information

5.24 Chapter 8 lays out a broad strategy for co-ordinating and developing information for individuals across health and social care. In addition, we propose that services **give all people with long-term health and social care needs and their carers an 'information prescription',** which we are currently developing. The information prescription will be given to people using services and their carers by health and social care professionals (for example GPs, social workers and district nurses) to signpost people to further information and advice to help them take care of their own condition.

5.25 By 2008, we would expect everyone with a long-term condition and/or long-term need for support – and their carers – to routinely receive information about their condition and, where they can, to receive peer and other self care support through networks.

Better assessment and care planning

5.26 People have told us that they would like greater integration between different services. A Common

UK best practice – joint working in Scotland

Joint Future is the Scottish policy on joint working between local authorities and the NHS in community care. The Joint Future Unit is charged with developing, implementing and monitoring policy. After initially focusing on systems such as Single Shared Assessment (SSA), the emphasis is now on outcomes, with partnerships demonstrating through Local Improvement Targets (LITs) how they are meeting the national outcomes.

Examples of good practice include:
- faster access to services and more holistic assessment through full implementation of SSA, with electronic information sharing and substantial access to resources across agency boundaries (North Lanarkshire);

- faster access to equipment through an integrated occupational therapy service with electronic, direct access to joint store (Fife);

- outcome-led, whole-system working, with joint management and joint resourcing of services (Glasgow);

- faster decision making through budgets being delegated to frontline staff (Aberdeenshire).

Assessment Framework is in place for children's services. We have already developed a Single Assessment Process for older people's services. Work is underway to build on this to develop a Common Assessment Framework to ensure less duplication across different agencies and allow people to self-assess where possible.[4] An integrated health and social care information system for shared care is planned as part of the NHS Connecting for Health strategy. It is an essential requirement for effective care co-ordination.

5.27 An integrated health and social care information system will enable a shared health and social care plan to follow a person as they move through the care system. **We will ensure that, ultimately, everyone who requires and wants one has a personal health and social care plan as part of an integrated health and social care record.** Initially we will focus on offering integrated care plans to those individuals who have complex health and social care needs. **By 2008 we would expect everyone with both long-term health and social care needs to have an integrated care plan if they want one. By 2010 we would expect everyone with a long-term condition to be offered a care plan.** We will issue good practice guidance early in 2007.

Integrated care for those with complex needs

5.28 Improving the health and care of people with complex longer-term needs is a major challenge for the health and social care system. Success would bring relief to a large number of people who in the past have had a high burden of suffering. And as this group is a significant user of the health service, both of primary and secondary care, success here could bring better health outcomes with a more effective use of resources too. It would mean that far more people could be helped to live independently at home or be treated in local community facilities – as most say they would prefer – and far fewer would suffer episodic health crises or be held for long periods in hospitals.

5.29 Where needs are complex, it is essential to identify a skilled individual who can act as a case manager and organise and co-ordinate services from a wide source of providers, following the guidance set out in the National Service Frameworks and the NHS and social care long-term conditions model.

5.30 An estimated 250,000 people with complex needs would benefit from case management, as required by the current Personal Service Agreements (PSA) target for long-term conditions.[5] This target is only the start and will require continual improvement once achieved. The current commitment to 3,000 community matrons, which is already part of the local delivery plans (LDPs), will help

deliver the skilled workforce required to support this group. Social workers and occupational therapists have always played major roles in this area of work and will continue to do so.

5.31 We will encourage the creation of multi-disciplinary networks and teams at PCT and local authority level. They will use a Common Assessment Framework, with prompt and ongoing access to an appropriate level of specialist expertise for diagnosis, treatment and follow-up where necessary. They need to operate on a sufficiently large geographic scale to ensure the involvement of all the key players, including social services, housing, and NHS primary, voluntary, community and secondary care services. These teams will also need to work closely with existing community palliative care teams.

5.32 By 2008 we expect all PCTs and local authorities to have established joint health and social care managed networks and/or teams to support those people with long-term conditions who have the most complex needs. Models for this can already be seen in mental health and intermediate care teams. In mental health, the Care Programme Approach will be reviewed during 2006 with the aim of improving consistency of approach and practice.

5.33 People with complex care needs require a single point of contact to mobilise support if there is an unexpected change in their needs or

They can use modern technology and web links to share information; technology is not being used to its full potential.

PARTICIPANT AT THE CITIZENS' SUMMIT IN BIRMINGHAM

CASE STUDY

Integrated care in West Sussex

People with complex needs require an integrated service, involving support from both health and social care professionals. Western Sussex PCT and West Sussex County Council (WSCC) are working in partnership with district councils and the voluntary and community sector to do just that through the Innovation Forum: Reducing Hospital Admissions project.

The main objective is to redesign care for older people with long-term chronic or complex health conditions around their needs and priorities, rather than around historic service models and professional roles. The project is being implemented in three sites, based in Bognor Regis, Selsey and the Midhurst rural area, and comprises a number of initiatives, which focus on providing care close to people's homes.

The partners have established an intensive care at home service, which integrates intensive nursing, health therapies and hospital-at-home services with social and caring services home care service providing care for up to six weeks.

"This way is so much better. I'm getting more individual treatment, I'm eating better and I'm sleeping better than I was in hospital. In a hospital ward, you are just one name among many. At home you are getting personalised health care. The care staff who come here have more time for me than they would do in hospital." Hip replacement patient, home within five days of receiving treatment

Importantly, the partners are also listening to what people are saying they want and have used innovative ways of engaging with local older people and voluntary and community sector providers. They have organised knowledge cafés which provide an informal café-style atmosphere where people feel relaxed and able to express their needs and concerns.

"The Innovation Forum project has encouraged creative thinking, in particular about social enterprise, which offers a new way to help local communities find their own solutions to meeting the needs of their vulnerable people". WSCC, Voluntary Sector Liaison Development Officer

a failure in agreed service provision. Further work needs to be done to establish how this can be achieved on a 24/7 basis by, for example, linking case management with out-of-hours services.

Disabled children

5.34 Many severely disabled children have health conditions requiring long-term management and/or nursing care and require help with the everyday activities of life such as bathing, feeding and toileting. The Department of Health will work with the

Department for Education and Skills and other stakeholders to implement the standard on disabled children in the National Service Framework for children, young people and maternity services and the recommendations in the Prime Minister's Strategy Unit report, *Improving the Life Chances of Disabled People*, to improve the support for disabled children and their families and to provide advice and support for disabled young people making the transition to adult services.

5.35 Drawing on the experience of key workers for disabled children, *Every Child Matters: Change for Children* recognised the importance of a named professional carrying out a co-ordinating role and contained proposals for a lead professional for children with additional needs to enable more children to experience this type of support. The lead professional role is intended to support those children who do not already have a keyworker or a professional from a statutory service overseeing co-ordination of their

care/support. More detail can be found in the *Lead Professional Good Practice Guidance for children with additional needs*[6] and the *Common Assessment Framework for Children and Young People: Guide for Service Managers and Practitioners*.[7]

Pointing the way to the future

5.36 There is now good international evidence, supported by small scale pilots in this country, that really dramatic improvements in the care of those with complex needs – including significant reductions in the use of unpopular hospital-based care – can be achieved. For example, the Veterans Health Administration in the United States has achieved dramatic improvements in care through its TELeHEART programme for veterans with high risk of cardiovascular disease. Through a comprehensive approach, with a strong focus both on helping people to help themselves and use of remote health technologies, there were significant improvements in health outcomes and far higher patient satisfaction, as well as substantial reductions in hospital use – admissions down 66 per cent, bed days of care down 71 per cent and emergency visits down 40 per cent.

5.37 Our challenge is to demonstrate on a wider scale that this significant shift from hospital care is now possible and that more people can be supported to retain their independence in the community. We need to provide credible evidence that it will benefit the individual and their carer's quality of life, and deliver gains in cost-effectiveness of care.

5.38 In doing so, we need to take full advantage of the exciting new possibilities opened up by assistive technologies. Many local authorities in this country have already shown that assistive technology can help people retain their independence and improve their quality of life. This capacity has been strengthened by an allocation of £80 million to local authorities over the next two years as part of the Preventative Technologies Grant. This will enable social services authorities to support even more people in their own homes by using telecare.

5.39 For example, remote monitoring enables people to have a different relationship with the health and social care system. It enables people to feel constantly supported at home, rather than left alone, reliant on occasional home visits or their capacity to access local services.

5.40 So for people with complex health and social care needs, we plan to bring together knowledge of what works internationally, with a powerful commitment to new, assistive technologies to demonstrate major improvements in care. This demonstration will include:

- a strong emphasis on patient education and empowerment, so that people are fully informed about their condition and are better able to manage it;

The future is now
Assistive technology already in use in or near the home, includes:
- house alarms linked to a call centre staffed by a nurse, co-ordinated by the local council;
- 'Well Elderly Clinics' for people living on their own but requiring some simple monitoring, including blood pressure, heart rate and glucose measurements;
- local intermediate care programmes that provide in-home support during recovery, aim to prevent unnecessary acute admission and maximise independence;
- spirometric and cardiac readings from in the home to detect acute episodes early and minimise or eliminate the need for hospitalisation – currently in place for chronic obstructive pulmonary disease, cardiac and pulmonary patients in limited geographies;
- in-home touch-screen and video link-up for patients to self-monitor and feed information to health professionals;
- bed sensors that determine if the resident has failed to return to bed by a set time.

- comprehensive and integrated packages of personalised health and social care services, including systematic chronic disease management programmes;

- joint health and social care teams, with dedicated case management through a single expert case manager, 24/7 service contact and an information system that supports a shared health and social care record;
- good local community health and care facilities, offering a better environment for the care of people with complex needs, and greater involvement of specialist nurses in care;
- health and social care commissioners with the right incentives to deliver better care for those with complex needs, mandatory risk stratification so that they can identify those most at risk, and accountability for their performance in improving the lives of those with complex needs;
- intensive use of assistive and home monitoring technologies.

5.41 These demonstrations will be challenged to achieve significant gains in quality of life and reductions in acute hospital use. We will work with a number of NHS, social care, private and voluntary sector partners, including NHS Connecting for Health and NHS Direct, to establish them. We will ensure that the resident population covered is at least 1 million and from a variety of geographical contexts so that gains are on a credible scale, and we will motivate all commissioners to drive services in this direction. The project will provide an opportunity to pilot a shared health and social care record. We aim to commence this

demonstration project by the end of 2006 and share early findings by the end of 2008.

5.42 We shall carry out this project in close collaboration with the Department of Trade and Industry so that the findings can inform a joint approach to our work with business and the research community to develop technology that will better meet the challenges identified.

A balanced scorecard approach

5.43 We will develop a balanced scorecard to provide a comprehensive and meaningful assessment of progress against many of the commitments outlined. This will be more outcome-focused and will draw on feedback from the people using services. It will also benchmark relative use of community and voluntary sector providers. In time, we expect to make use of outcome measures to assess the impact and effectiveness of services and new service models. We will make the scorecard available to PCTs, practices and local authorities for local use.

Incentives for better care for people with longer-term needs

5.44 The reforms described recently in *Health reform in England*[8] will provide a fundamental underpinning to improvements in the care of those with longer-term needs. Under PBC, primary care professionals will control the majority of health care resources through indicative budgets and be able to use them accordingly. Payment by Results (PBR) makes real to commissioners the benefits of improving care for people with long-term needs, by making clear the costs of preventable illnesses, avoidable emergency admissions, poor medication prescription and use, and lack of preventative investment in social care. The combination of PBC and PBR will encourage commissioners to seek out providers who offer better quality care, particularly for those that are the most intensive users of health care.

5.45 To do this, commissioners will often need to work with a range of local providers to develop comprehensive, integrated and more effective packages of care. For all parties to develop such packages and to share the benefits from this improved care, co-operation will often be needed. The national tariff,

currently for activity in an acute setting, provides the transparent financial framework within which such co-operation and benefit sharing between commissioners and providers can be negotiated for care delivered in primary and community care. To ensure this is as effective as possible, **we will explore whether there are refinements to the current tariff that could provide incentives for such benefit sharing, to support co-operation between commissioners and providers in delivering integrated long-term conditions care.**

5.46 We will examine carefully the 'year of care approach' that is currently being developed for people with diabetes. In so doing we will bear in mind the fact that there will be a year of care for commissioners at local level

Figure 5.3 Carers by age and sex

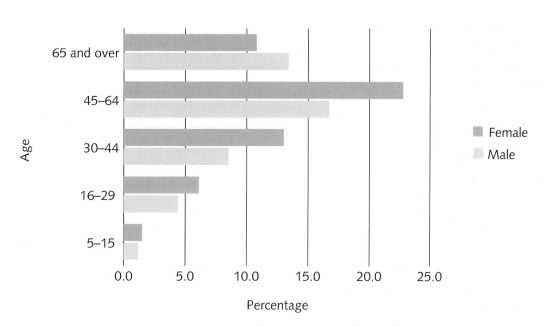

Source: Census, April 2001, Office for National Statistics.

Figure 5.4 Carers by profession

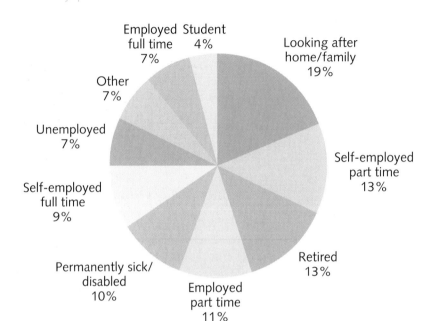

Source: Census, April 2001, Office for National Statistics

through practice based budgets, that PBC is designed to give flexibility as to how those budgets are best deployed and that people with long-term conditions often have co-morbidities and multiple needs that are not easily disaggregated into discrete conditions.

5.47 We will also work with NHS Employers and the professions to explore how the QOF can continue to develop to provide stronger incentives for effective management of people with long-term conditions, building on the recent agreement for 2006/07.

Investing in professional education and skills development

5.48 We will take action at each stage of the professional education and regulatory process to change the underlying culture profoundly and encourage support for individuals' empowerment and self care. **We will be taking forward work that not only creates a clear self care competency framework for staff, but also embeds key elements, including values and behaviours around assessment and support in appraisal and continuing professional development requirements. This will include:**

- work with Skills for Health and Skills for Care to develop a self care competency framework for all staff;
- work with NHS Employers to embed self care in the Knowledge and Skills Framework, so that it is embedded in job descriptions/ annual appraisals under Agenda for Change;

CASE STUDY

Who cares for carers?

If you are a carer it can be difficult to respond to an urgent problem, such as your own health failing. When someone depends on you, you can't just drop everything. However, the Carers Emergency Respite Team (CERT) in Sefton on Merseyside has pioneered a unique service offering an instant response when a carer faces an emergency that would stop them being able to continue caring.

Dilwyn James, Development Manager at Sefton Carers Centre, says that: "Team members can be at a carer's home within an hour of them calling us." A pre-briefed member of the CERT team steps in and provides emergency respite care.

But the Carers Centre is not just for an emergency. Dilwyn says: "We have a broad range of services here at the centre, such as

therapies to help deal with stress and counselling support, and we offer advice on welfare rights for the whole family."

There is also a sitting service so that a carer can go to the hairdresser's or to lunch with friends.

- work with the professional bodies to embed self care in core curricula.

A new deal for carers

5.49 There are 6 million carers in this country. Caring for someone can have life-altering consequences. People caring more than 50 hours a week (1.25 million people) are twice as likely not to be in good health as those who are not carers. Three-quarters of carers are financially worse off because of

their caring responsibilities. In addition, 400,000 people combine full time work with caring more than 20 hours per week.

5.50 The *Your health, your care, your say* listening exercise revealed considerable public support for carers. Better support for carers came third in the 'people's options' at the national Citizens' Summit.

5.51 We therefore propose to offer a new deal for carers to improve support for them through a range of measures.

5.52 We will **update and extend the Prime Minister's 1999 Strategy for Carers and encourage councils and PCTs to nominate leads for carers' services.** The updated strategy will reflect developments in carers' rights, direct payment regulations, carers' assessment and carers' grants. We will work with stakeholders to consult, develop and issue a revised cross-government strategy that promotes the health and well-being of carers, including the particular needs of younger carers, and includes the use of universal services.

5.53 **We will establish an information service/helpline for carers, perhaps run by a voluntary organisation.** Carers have difficulty accessing the right up-to-date information to assist them in their caring role. They need reliable, detailed information to help them make decisions about their personal support, opportunities for them and the needs of the person for whom they care.

5.54 A dedicated helpline for carers would offer information in the widest sense – from legal entitlements, to contact numbers for 'help' groups and training, to advice on benefits.

5.55 **In each council area, we will ensure that short-term, home-based respite support is established for carers in crisis or emergency situations.**

5.56 **We will also allocate specific funding for the creation of an Expert Carers Programme.** Similar to the EPP, this will provide training for carers to develop the skills they need to take greater control over their own health, and the health of those in their care.

NHS Continuing Care

5.57 Finally, during 2006, as part of care planning between the NHS and social care, we will support NHS and social care professionals' decision making on responsibility (and funding) through a national framework for NHS-funded continuing care and nursing care. This will provide clarity and consistency for both patients and professionals about what the NHS will provide for those with the most complex long-term care needs. We will also clarify how the NHS Continuing Care strategy should work for children.

References

1   National Service Frameworks for Coronary Heart Disease, Diabetes, Long-Term Conditions, Mental Health, Renal Services and the NHS Cancer Plan

2   *Supporting people with long-term conditions. An NHS and Social Care Model to support local innovation and integration*, Department of Health, January 2005

3   Wittenberg, Pickard, Comas-Herrera, Financing Long-Term Care for Older People, *PSSRU Bulletin* No.14, 1999

4   A Common Assessment Framework for children and young people has already been developed and is being used by health practitioners for children with additional needs

5   The PSA target includes promises to improve health outcomes by offering personalised care plans for people most at risk, and to reduce emergency bed days by 5 per cent by improving care in primary and community settings by 2008

6   *Lead Professional Good Practice Guidance for children with additional needs*, Department for Education and Skills, July 2005

7   *Common Assessment Framework for Children and Young People: Guide for Service Managers and Practitioners*, Department for Education and Skills, March 2005

8   *Health reform in England: Update and next steps*, Department of Health, December 2005

CHAPTER 6

Care closer to home

Care closer to home

This chapter on care closer to home includes:

- shifting care within particular specialties into community settings;
- the need over time for growth in health spending to be directed more towards preventative, primary, community and social care services;
- a new generation of community hospitals, to provide a wider range of health and social care services in a community setting;
- a review of service reconfiguration and consultation to streamline processes and accelerate the development of facilities for care closer to home;
- refining the tariff to provide stronger incentives for practices and Primary Care Trusts (PCTs) to develop more primary and community services;
- accurate and timely information for the public on specialist services available in a community setting.

The need for change

6.1 Twentieth-century health and social care was rooted in institutions and dependence. In the large specialist hospital offering more complex treatment than a GP could provide, or in the residential complex, which accommodated groups needing more support, people were too often seen as passive recipients of care.

6.2 In future, far more care will be provided in more local and convenient settings. People want this, and changes in technology and clinical practice are making it safer and more feasible.

- People's expectations have changed dramatically. People want greater independence, more choice and more control. They want a service that does not force them to plan their lives around multiple visits to large, hectic sites, or force them to present the same information to different professionals.
- Technology is changing: clinical activity that in the past was provided in hospitals can now be undertaken locally and safely. The way to do it is to plan the patient pathway so that specialist skills are integrated into it.
- As the population ages over the coming decades, it will impose ever greater demands on the health care system – as Wanless has shown.[1] A strategy centred on high-cost hospitals will be inefficient and unaffordable compared to one focused on prevention and supporting individual well-being in the community.
- With increases in expenditure slowing down after 2008, following record increases over the past few years, the health service will need to focus even more strongly on delivering better care with better value for money. Finding new ways to provide services, in more local settings, will be one way to meet this challenge.

Specialist care more locally

6.3 Care is delivered closer to home in many other countries. For instance, Germany has virtually no outpatient appointments carried out in hospitals. We have looked at the lessons we can learn from international best practice: patient pathways that put more focus on providing care closer to home can improve outcomes for people, be more cost-effective, and improve people's satisfaction. Yet at present we spend 27 per cent of our budget on primary care services, compared with an OECD average of 33 per cent.

6.4 There is also good evidence from England that a wide range of clinical activity could be safely and effectively provided outside the acute hospital.

6.5 For example, a report last year by Professor Sir Ara Darzi, Professor of Surgery at both Imperial College and St Mary's Hospital, London, working with an expert advisory group, identified a large number of procedures

In several countries, including Australia, France, Germany and Switzerland, many specialists provide services outside hospital. In Germany, polyclinics – under the re-branded name of Medizinische Versorgungszentren (MVZ, medical care centres) – were re-introduced to the health care system in 2004. The renewed interest in polyclinics among policy-makers has been stimulated by their potential to enhance co-ordination of care. A minimum of two physicians from different specialties are required to set up an MVZ. Teams usually include at least one general practitioner but can also involve nurses, pharmacists, psychotherapists or psychiatrists, as well as other health care professionals.

Additionally, the MVZs are free to contract with other health-related organisations (for example those providing home-based care).

Another well-known example of integrated care closer to home is Kaiser Permanente in the US. Kaiser uses far fewer acute bed days in relation to the population served than the NHS, and 3.5 times fewer bed days for the 11 leading causes of bed days in the NHS. Lengths of stay are more important than admission rates in explaining these differences. Lower utilisation of acute bed days is achieved through integration of care, active management of patients, the use of intermediate care, self care and medical leadership.[2]

which would allow patient admission for a short stay outside the acute hospital, without the need for on-site critical care. Procedures would be performed either by consultants, trainees, GPs or allied heath professionals. This has formed the basis for the development of treatment centres.

6.6 From the outset it needs to be clear that the rationale behind providing care closer to home is based on the better use of highly specialist skills – not on a dilution of them. We want to see specialists fully engaged locally as partners in designing new patient pathways. The key feature of a

patient-centred approach is that specialist assessment is available speedily, from professionals with the right training, and in the right place. This may or may not be the consultant and may or may not be in a hospital.

6.7 Care closer to home also requires appropriate diagnostic and other equipment in local settings. For example, if breast assessment were to be located outside the hospital service, access would be needed to mammography, ultrasound and needle biopsy facilities. Provision of this sort of equipment is a key focus of the current diagnostic procurement programme, and delivering access to these facilities locally is a critical component in meeting the 18-week waiting time target.

6.8 Practice Based Commissioning (PBC) and patient choice will be pivotal vehicles for making these changes happen. Using indicative budgets, practices will be able to see clearly how the overall health spend on new patients is being used; they will then have the scope to redesign care pathways to match patients' needs and wishes.

6.9 The challenge is to make best practice in the NHS the norm, rather than the exception. Shifting care has to be evidence-based. In some cases in the past it has led to more fractured, less holistic care, as well as being more expensive to provide. Past models associated with GP fund-holding – with specialists seeing small numbers of patients in GP surgeries – should be ruled out.

6.10 To ensure a stronger evidence base and real clinical engagement, **the Department of Health is working with**

CASE STUDY

Keeping it flowing in the Fens

The Fenland Anticoagulation Nursing Service (FANS) was formed in August 2001 to address inequalities in anticoagulation care. The service is funded by East Cambridgeshire and Fenland Primary Care Trust (PCT). FANS now covers 423 square miles and is staffed by specialist anticoagulation nurses who see all patients who need medication to stop their blood clotting.

FANS provides its services in a variety of settings: community hospital-based clinics, GP surgery-based clinics and home visits to the housebound and nursing home residents. Nurses can test patients on-site and will know the results within minutes.

The specialist nurse can provide medication on-site using computerised technology. Peter Carré is delighted with the service: "I've been taking anticoagulants since I had a heart valve replacement in 1975, and for most of that time I've had to make long journeys to hospitals and sometimes wait for hours to be seen.

"The new service is fantastic. My blood is tested on the spot, I'm in and out quickly, and when I had another heart valve replacement last June the nurse came to see me at home a few times until I was well enough to attend the appointments. This new system is so much more efficient – it saves time and hassle and has really changed things for me."

Development plans are underway to expand the service to prevent hospital admissions for Deep Vein Thrombosis (DVT) patients. The aim is to diagnose and treat in the community all 'in scope' patients with a suspected diagnosis of DVT.

the specialty associations and the Royal Colleges to define clinically safe pathways that provide the right care in the right setting, with the right equipment, performed by the appropriate skilled person.

6.11 Leading the way in looking at models for providing care closer to home are six specialties – ear, nose and throat, trauma and orthopaedics, dermatology, urology, gynaecology and general surgery. **Over the next 12 months the Department of Health will work with these specialties in demonstration sites to define the appropriate models of care that can be used nationwide, based on the models described below.**

6.12 We will investigate a number of models of care, including the use of trained professionals like specialist nurses, speech therapists, health care scientists and GPwSIs. The demonstrations will consider issues such as clinical governance and infrastructure requirements. Bodies such as the NHS Institute for Innovation and Improvement will be involved in developing and evaluating these demonstrations as appropriate.

6.13 Practices and PCTs will then be responsible for commissioning services for these and subsequent specialties, using the recommended models of delivery. The Integrated Service Improvement Programme (ISIP) will help to support this, working closely with PCTs as commissioners and with providers of care.

CASE STUDY

Care closer to home, better for patients

In **Bradford**, the general practitioner with a special interest (GPwSI) service is used for at least 60 per cent of all GP referrals (GPs can refer urgent cases directly to consultants). This encourages (but does not require) the use of the specialist triage service. A quality marker monitors use of the service, and there is a further marker that has helped to control overall referral growth: a practice's overall dermatology referrals should not go up by more than 2 per cent per annum.

Within the **Greater Manchester** Strategic Health Authority (SHA), a model for Tier 2 services – intermediate health care services which provide aspects of secondary care to patients in primary care settings – has been implemented. Starting with orthopaedics, which had long waiting times, referrals to Tier 2 services were made mandatory. Greater Manchester SHA demonstrated a relationship between increased Tier 2 referrals and a decrease in secondary care referrals, thus demonstrating shifting care. As an example, Bolton PCT's musclo-skeletal GP referrals to consultants were reduced by 40 per cent in 12 months. At the same time, conversion rates (ie the proportion of outpatients admitted to hospital) increased from 20 per cent to between 50 and 60 per cent, reflecting the fact that consultants were seeing more serious cases.

In **Stockport**, responding to long waiting times for vasectomies, a GPwSI service was set up by two GPwSIs. Patients were waiting up to 11 months from GP referral to local anaesthetic vasectomy, and the 'did not appear' rate for this procedure was high. The GPwSIs were trained, with re-accreditation provided by a lead urology consultant. Referrals are directed to the patient information centre, where patients are able to choose their appointment date and time. All patients are offered a procedure date within six weeks of their referral. Within the first nine months of the service commencing, 288 procedures were undertaken within six weeks, with only three onward referrals. This service has reduced the total day-case waiting time for urology by 45 per cent. The cost per case has been reduced from £463 to £150.

In **Exeter**, a team of audiology health care scientists provide direct access to diagnostic, monitoring and treatment services in primary care. Previously, patients would have been referred to the ear, nose and throat (ENT) outpatients department, with a wait of up to 18 months for a consultation. Now only clinically appropriate cases are referred to ENT, reducing the referral rate by 90 per cent. In a 12-month period 2,900 paediatric hearing tests were carried out by audiology health care scientists which would previously have been done by a community paediatrician. Children can now be treated in six weeks, as opposed to six months.

In **Somerset**, a team of health care scientists in a community hospital are running a diagnostic service for urinary tract infections. The patients are tested and treated appropriately on the same day, with a reduction in referrals to secondary care of 85 per cent. Before the service started, 66 per cent of patients were receiving unnecessary antibiotics, whereas now only 11 per cent receive antibiotics for proven infection.

Specialty	Model of care
Dermatology	• Wherever possible, patients with long-term skin conditions such as psoriasis and eczema should be managed by appropriately trained specialists in convenient community settings and should be able to re-access specialist services as and when needed. • Many specialist dermatology units already provide up to 30 per cent of their services in community settings, usually in well-equipped community hospitals. This type of service should be encouraged wherever possible. • PwSIs and specialist dermatology nurses can have an important role in providing care close to home for patients with skin disease. Health communities should develop these services where they are not already in place.
ENT	• Where appropriate, otitis externa and rhinitis are suitable for GP/PwSi management in the community. • The use of multi-disciplinary teams, including scientists, should be increased both within and outside the hospital setting. • There is the potential for appropriate day-case surgery to be performed in community hospitals where patient volumes justify recurrent and capital costs.
General surgery	• Where appropriate, specialised clinics should be established in the community, for example rectal bleeding clinics. • PwSI-led services, such as varicose vein and inguinal hernia clinics, are suitable for local, out-of-hospital settings (dependent on local need). • The more efficient use of current operating facilities and intermediate-care step-down facilities can improve quality outcomes and improve patient satisfaction.

Specialty	Model of care
Orthopaedics	• With suitable diagnostics, there is potential to shift up to 40 per cent of outpatient consultations to the out-of-hospital setting. This shift could take place through both the transfer of care to non-specialist health care professionals working in collaboration with the orthopaedic consultant, and through orthopaedic surgeons providing care in the out-of-hospital setting. • The use of intermediate, setting step-down care can free up hospital beds, thus improving surgical efficiency.
Urology	• There is a large potential for new pathways, and to involve suitably trained non-specialists in the management and treatment of certain conditions. • Where appropriate, and with suitable diagnostic support, male and female bladder dysfunction, stones and andrology can be locally managed in the community.
Gynaecology	• Where appropriate, non-specialist health care professionals can perform out-of-hospital management, investigations and treatment for certain conditions, such as infertility, menorrhagia and menstrual problems. • Self-referral to specialist infertility clinics, as evidence suggests that 90 per cent of presentations to primary care are referred on to specialists.

6.14 The purpose of the demonstrations will be to redesign care pathways so that they offer safe and effective care in settings that people want. There is already activity underway in the NHS in this area. So the demonstrations in the specialties will focus on particular parts of the care pathway, specifically on outpatient appointments, outpatient follow-ups, day-case surgery and step-down care.

6.15 Currently there are nearly 45 million outpatient appointments every year in England. Estimates vary by specialty, but for some specialties up to half of these could eventually be provided in a community setting.

6.16 There is also evidence of huge variation in performance across the NHS. While some of this may be explainable, the demonstrations will

Figure 6.1: Scope for shifting care

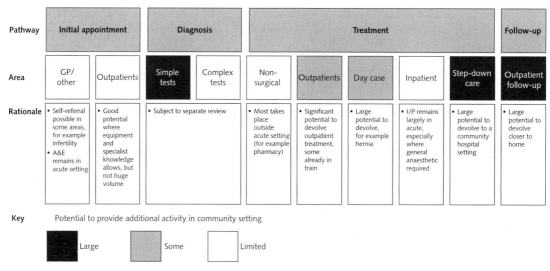

Pathway	Initial appointment		Diagnosis		Treatment					Follow-up
Area	GP/other	Outpatients	Simple tests	Complex tests	Non-surgical	Outpatients	Day case	Inpatient	Step-down care	Outpatient follow-up
Rationale	• Self-referral possible in some areas, for example infertility • A&E remains in acute setting	• Good potential where equipment and specialist knowledge allows, but not huge volume	• Subject to separate review		• Most takes place outside acute setting (for example pharmacy)	• Significant potential to devolve outpatient treatment, some already in train	• Large potential to devolve, for example hernia	• I/P remains largely in acute, especially where general anaesthetic required	• Large potential to devolve to a community hospital setting	• Large potential to devolve closer to home

Key Potential to provide additional activity in community setting

■ Large ▨ Some □ Limited

Source: Department of Health analysis

seek to determine suitable clinical protocols to eliminate unnecessary attendances. Doing this alone could save patients from having to make up to one million costly and unnecessary trips to hospital.

6.17 Alternatively, parts of the pathway could be redesigned. For example, there is the potential for having a simple follow-up assessment performed by a nurse, by a suitably trained community worker or indeed via a telephone call where appropriate. We will explore whether this approach would be able to swiftly identify problems, save wasted journeys for patients, and make non-attendance by patients less likely.

6.18 In addition, the demonstrations will look at the potential for 'step-down' beds to allow for recuperation in community settings. Today there are 5,000 intermediate care beds jointly

funded by health and social care. The demonstration in orthopaedics, especially, will examine the potential to make better use of these beds, helping patients to recover faster in a more appropriate setting and, working with social care, giving them back the skills needed to live independently at home.

6.19 The potential to replace acute bed days with less intensive beds is considerable. Best practice produced by the NHS Institute under the Integrated Service Improvement Programme (ISIP) programme shows that these acute beds could be released if better use is made of intermediate care beds.

6.20 Frail older people rely particularly on what are called 'intermediate care' facilities. These are in the community, outside acute hospitals, and they enable people who strongly value their independence to access more support than is available at home ('step-up').

Figure 6.2 Median, low and top decile SHA performance for outpatients (O/P)

	O/P appointments	O/P appointments per 1,000 population			Ratio of initial to follow-up appointments		
	Q4 2004/05	Low decile	Median	Top decile	Low decile	Median	Top decile
Dermatology	525,773	2.89	3.70	4.82	1.53	1.82	2.41
ENT	559,046	3.76	4.46	5.60	1.26	1.44	1.74
Urology	366,707	1.77	2.25	2.66	1.82	2.36	2.69
Trauma and orthopaedics	1,334,696	7.76	9.44	11.27	1.61	1.88	2.32
General surgery	827,695	5.36	6.59	8.49	1.26	1.56	1.78
Obstetrics and gynaecology	581,079	4.00	4.86	6.74	1.06	1.27	1.74
TOTAL	4,194,996						

NB data is for one quarter only. 'Low decile' refers to the SHA with the third-lowest figure (out of 28).
Source: HES Data, Q4 2005

These facilities also enable people to leave the acute hospital and to get ready to return home ('step-down').

6.21 For instance, hip fractures account for 945,847 acute bed days every year,[3] or around 2,600 acute beds at any one time. These acute beds could be released if better use is made of intermediate care beds. Local intermediate care is good for the patient – it is often closer to relatives – and evidence has shown that care standards are higher. Intermediate care should be supported by tight integration of health and social care services to support patients in getting home as speedily as possible.

6.22 Our strategic approach to shifting care requires PCTs, together with their partners, to mobilise the total investment across the locality to ensure that it is used to best effect. Stays in hospital can be significantly reduced and independent living at home can be supported provided that funds are mobilised and provided that the right specialist input is available. Hospitals can then devote themselves to meeting the clinical needs that they are uniquely equipped to meet.

Getting people back home in Peterborough

Peterborough has very integrated services. Since April 2004 the budgets of two PCTs and of the adult social care department of the city council have been fully pooled. Since spring 2005 district nursing and social work staff have been part of fully integrated teams.

These joined-up services are already making a difference to people in Peterborough. At the end of last year, 92-year-old Eve Vaughan was treated in hospital for an intestinal blockage. Her left wrist was already in plaster following a fall. The treatment was successful, but Mrs Vaughan wouldn't have been able to care for herself at home. The integrated transfer of care team arranged for her to move to an interim care bed at Greenwood House, one of Peterborough local authority's residential care homes.

"I couldn't possibly have looked after myself," explains Mrs Vaughan. "I think this was a good idea for me, because I'm on my feet. I've been very well looked after and very comfortable, and the carers come to help you if you need them."

"It's a small unit and we have more time," says care assistant Herma Whyte. "We can see that they're eating properly, and can walk with them for a short distance at a time. They feel more confident, and can see what progress they're making. We're here to help them get back home, which is what everyone wants."

6.23 There are likely to be around 20 to 30 demonstration sites over the next 12 months. Leading clinicians, their teams, their PCTs and local councils will work together to ensure that these sites are providing transferred care, and not simply creating demand for new types of services. They will also be responsible for ensuring that commissioners are not 'double-paying' for care outside hospital settings. **The Department of Health will fund an overall programme to evaluate and report results on a consistent basis across all these demonstrations, while funding for the delivery of care itself will continue to be provided by practices and PCTs, as at present.**

6.24 These demonstrations are expected to highlight the effectiveness of new models of care compared to those offered at present. They will then provide the strength of evidence to give practices and PCTs what they need to commit to fundamental service redesign and to the development of more local models of care. The demonstrations support national policy development in a number of areas through the:

*   production of recommended care pathways for potential use in National Framework contracts, in the NHS Connecting for Health Map of Medicine resource, and in supporting community hospital service specifications, including social care elements;

- development of a tariff using best practice, rather than current national averages. For example, a tariff where components are related to the cost of care or treatment in the community rather than in acute settings;

- production of stretching but fair targets or performance measures for PCTs, relating to the overall share of activity undertaken in primary and community versus secondary settings;

- description of multi-skilled models to determine future workforce requirements more precisely.

Shifting resources

6.25 In social care we have already made a clear statement to the effect that we want to focus on enabling people to retain their independence at home and in the community. One of the key aims – embodied in a Public Service Agreement – is to increase the number of people supported intensively to live at home to 34 per cent of the total number of those being supported by social services at home or in residential care. Local authorities are on track to achieve this by 2007/08. In 2004/05, 32 per cent of people receiving intensive care support did so in their own homes.

6.26 For some people, residential care may be the best option, but we want to ensure that, wherever possible, people have the option to stay in their own homes. Greater use of community services including extra-care housing,

intermediate care services, community equipment, intensive support at home and support for carers, has enabled more people to be cared for closer to home and to continue to live in their own homes for longer.

6.27 We will build on this in order to improve the well-being of older people and their families. We are already working across Government to improve the delivery of home adaptations, linking this closely with the Integrated Community Equipment Service. The Office of the Deputy Prime Minister's Disabled Facilities Grant programme helps to fund adaptations to enable older and disabled people to live as comfortably and independently as possible in their own homes. These adaptations include improving access in the home through ramps, stairlifts and level-access showers.

6.28 In addition, for those in residential care, the principles of retaining independence and opportunities for interaction and involvement with the wider community will remain fundamental.

6.29 Turning to the NHS, there has been an unprecedented increase in investment in hospitals. This has been right and proper and has resulted in huge reductions in waiting lists and times. The maximum wait for an operation is now six months, whereas it exceeded 18 months in 2000. By 2008 it will be just 18 weeks from GP referral to treatment. Meanwhile, the total number of patients waiting has been reduced by half a million.[4]

6.30 Yet participants in the *Your health, your care, your say* consultation said they wanted more care provided in community settings. The majority favoured increased investment in the latter, even if this meant changing the type and scale of services provided by their local hospital. Increased investment in primary care would also bring us into line with international experience.

6.31 Therefore, we want there to be an overall shift of resources from hospitals to care in community settings. Choice, tariff and PBC and PCT commissioning will all be important drivers of this shift. Locally, PCTs already have plans for

unprecedented high growth in their revenue over the next two years. Combined with the changes we are making to tariffs, this will, we expect, give local health communities the scope to move quickly where it makes sense locally. As a consequence, we should see spending on primary and community care begin to grow faster than spending on acute hospitals.

6.32 This shift of resource will need to happen in every part of the country. As NHS budgets continue to grow and the take-up of PBC increases, the percentage of each PCT's budget spent outside the current secondary care sector will be expected to rise. So:
* **for the 2008 planning round, PCT Local Delivery Plans will not be agreed by SHAs or the**

Figure 6.3 Citizens' Summit in favour of shifting care
"To what extent do you support or oppose providing more services closer to home, including community hospitals, if this means that some larger hospitals concentrate on specialist services and some merge or close?"

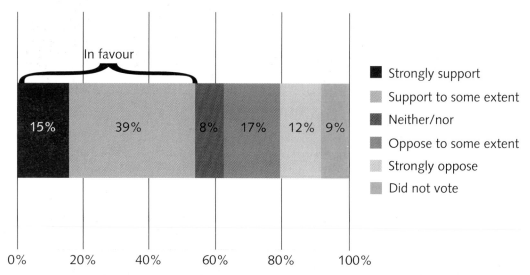

Figure 6.4 Spend on prevention and public health

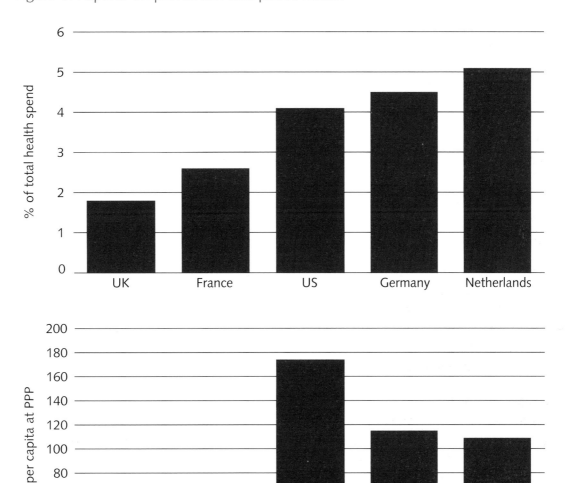

Source: OECD
Note: Prevention and public health services consist of services designed to enhance the health status of the population as opposed to the curative services which repair health dysfunction. Typical services are vaccination campaigns and programmes (function HC.6 in the International Classification for Health Accounts). 1999 data.

Department of Health unless there is a clear strategy for the development of primary and community care, including ambitious goals for the shift of resources rooted in the vision and agenda of this White Paper;

- from 2008 onwards, PCTs will be scrutinised annually against this strategy and these goals;

- **further, in preparation for the 2008 planning round, we will review the recent evolution of PCT budgets and will examine the case for setting a target for the percentage shift from current secondary care to primary and community care, if it is felt that such a target is needed to supplement health reform incentives and drivers.**

6.33 An increased commitment to spending on prevention should be part of the shift in resources from secondary to primary and community care. The UK spend on prevention and public health is relatively low compared to that of other advanced economies. Again, the new incentives and drivers of the health reform programme, and the policy agenda of this White Paper, should lead local primary care services and PCTs to increase their spend on prevention.

6.34 This is something that PCTs should be monitoring. At present, though, the definition and measurement of spend on prevention are not easy to apply. Spend on prevention and spend on public health should be separated more clearly. International and UK definitions of preventative and public health spend are not aligned, and issues like service quality are not adequately captured. So we will:

- **establish an expert group to develop robust definitions and measures of preventative health spending, to report later in 2006;**

- **implement these recommendations, to ensure that we have good data on preventative spend, for both PCT and international comparisons;**
- **use these data, and evidence on the prevention outcomes for the UK, to look at establishing a 10-year ambition for preventative spending, based on a comparison with other OECD countries.**

6.35 Following the development of better measures of preventative spending, we will then treat spending on prevention in the same manner as spending on primary and community care. So:

- for the 2008 planning round, PCT Local Delivery Plans will not be agreed by SHAs or the Department of Health unless there is a clear strategy for the development of preventative services, including setting an ambitious goal for a shift of resources to prevention, as set out in the vision and agenda of this White Paper;
- from 2008 onwards, PCTs will be scrutinised annually against this strategy and goal;
- further, in preparation for the 2008 planning round, we will review the recent evolution of PCT budgets and will examine the case for setting a target for the percentage shift in the share of resources spent on prevention.

Community facilities accessible to all

6.36 In order for specialist care to be delivered more locally, we will need to ensure that the necessary infrastructure is in place. This will mean developing a new generation of community facilities.

6.37 Investment in intermediate care and related community services since 2001 has already resulted in a reduction in delayed discharge from acute hospitals of 64 per cent by September 2005,[5] releasing about 1.5 million bed days per year. More than 360,000 people are receiving these services per annum. We intend to build on this so that more people benefit from supported early discharge, ensuring that opportunities for secondary prevention, treatment, rehabilitation, home adaptation, domiciliary care and support for carers are explored before a decision is taken about long-term placement in residential or nursing home care following a hospital admission. Strengthened intermediate care services will also provide safe and effective alternatives to acute hospital admission for many people.

6.38 We intend to fulfil the manifesto commitment to 'help create an even greater range of provision and further improve convenience, we will over the next five years develop a new generation of modern NHS community hospitals. These state-of-the-art centres will provide diagnostics, day surgery and outpatient facilities closer to where people live and work.'

6.39 These will be places where a wide range of health and social care services can work together to provide integrated services to the local community. They will complement more specialist hospitals, serving catchment areas of roughly 100,000 people, but taking on more complex procedures, for example complex surgery requiring general anaesthetic or providing fully-fledged accident and emergency facilities. They will be places where:

- health specialists work alongside generalists, skilled nursing staff and therapists to provide care covering less complex conditions;
- specialists provide clinics for patients, and mentoring and training for other professionals;
- patients will have speedy access to key diagnostic tests and where health care scientists may work in different ways;
- patients will get a range of elective day case and outpatient surgery for simpler procedures;
- patients are offered intermediate 'step-up' care to avoid unnecessary admissions, and 'step-down' care for recovering closer to home after treatment;
- patient self-help groups and peer networks provide support for people in managing their own health;

- social services are tightly integrated, providing a one-stop shop for people and helping them to access support in the home;
- patients can access the support they need for the management of their long-term conditions, including from case managers, community matrons and especially from each other;
- care is provided closer to home for the one fifth of the population who live a long way from an acute hospital;
- urgent care is provided during the day, and 'out of hours' is co-ordinated at night.

6.40 Evidence shows that there are a number of benefits of community hospitals, one of which is that they provide better recuperative care than District General Hospitals (DGHs).[6] Of the 11 leading causes of hospital bed use in the UK, eight are due to illnesses or conditions for which greater use of community facilities could lead to fewer patients needing to be in hospital or to be there for as long. The Kaiser Permanente model in the United States has also suggested that integrated care closer to home can reduce the length of hospital stays dramatically.[7] People have shown a preference for care closer to home to support them to manage their own condition.

6.41 There are many successful examples of thriving community hospitals providing many of these services today. It is estimated that there are 350 community hospitals in England, if we use the definition of a community hospital as 'a service which offers integrated health and social care and is supported by community-based professionals'.[8] Most of these are owned and run by PCTs.

6.42 Some community hospitals are currently under threat of closure, as PCTs consider the best configuration of services in their area. Where these closures are due to facilities that are clinically not viable or which local people do not want to use, then local reconfiguration is right. However, we are clear that community facilities should not be lost in response to short-term budgetary pressures that are not related to the viability of the community facility itself.

6.43 Indeed, this White Paper lays out a vision for a future in which we are likely to see far more expanded intermediate care. **So PCTs taking current decisions about the future of community hospitals will be required to demonstrate to their SHA that they have consulted locally and have considered options such as developing new pathways, new partnerships and new ownership possibilities. SHAs will then test PCT community hospital proposals against the principles of this White Paper.**

6.44 We will further invite interested PCTs, where appropriate working with local authority partners, to bid for capital support for reinvestment in the new generation of community

Thriving community hospitals

In **Paignton**, the local community hospital has been reformed so that care is now led by nurses and therapists, who do all admission and discharges. Medical cover is provided by a small team of GPs with a special interest in care of the elderly who work as one full-time equivalent, 9am to 5pm Monday to Friday. The community hospital has a focus on step-down care and works in partnership with the local DGH to provide services that are less intensive and less expensive. There are clear patient admittance criteria and patients must have a definite diagnosis or care plan. This helps to prevent excessive lengths of stay. Health and social care are fully integrated, with locality managers having dual responsibility for managing health and community staff.

In **Wiltshire**, Trowbridge Hospital has successfully developed a project to improve patient discharge planning and promote independence. Project goals include: no care home placements from hospital, to meet and exceed the target average length of hospital stay of 14 days, minimise delayed discharges: acute and community and reduce bed occupancy. Following a process mapping and redesign exercise by staff, a number of changes were made. An estimated discharge date was set within 24 hours of admission and prior to admission where possible, the multi-disciplinary team assessments to begin within 24 hours of admission, and the team having a daily handover. Additional investment in ward social work time was also made. As a result length of stay and readmission rates have fallen, and the number of local authority funded placements has significantly reduced.

hospitals and smaller facilities offering local, integrated health and social care services. This will provide the opportunity to create many new community hospitals, as we have done with LIFT projects, and to expand services on existing community hospital sites if more appropriate. The details of the timing and the tender process will be published in a separate document in mid-2006.

6.45 The tender process will require a comprehensive review of system provision across community and acute hospitals to determine the most appropriate method for delivery of care, as well as to demonstrate care provision closer to home, co-location of health and social services, integration of generalists and specialists, and plurality of provision (including third-sector).

6.46 New housing developments have an impact on primary care and community services – for example, immediate increases in demand for GP services. The Government will explore ways in which local planning authorities and local providers of health services can work together better, to ensure that the impacts of new developments on existing services are properly addressed through the planning system. **The NHS locally is encouraged to work closely with planning authorities; we are proposing to produce a guide to assist with this.**

Co-location

6.47 Central to this is the need for seamless joint delivery for the user of services. People do not care about organisational boundaries when seeking support or help, and expect services to reflect this. 'One-stop shops' are now commonplace features of the range of services offered by local authorities. We want to see greater integration, not only between the NHS and social care services, but also between other statutory agencies and services as well as the community and voluntary sectors.

6.48 Our vision is that people who access health and social care services should also be able to easily access other services such as benefits and employment advice – all from the same place. This is particularly important in the most disadvantaged areas, and we will need to build on the innovative approaches already being taken by healthy living centres, neighbourhood management initiatives and other local schemes.

6.49 Community hospitals offer one potential model for co-located health and social care services. The principle of co-locating different public services was endorsed in the *Your health, your care, your say* listening exercise. Over 70 per cent of respondents to the on-line questionnaire felt that being able to get advice and information from a GP, community nurse, social worker or housing or benefits adviser in one place would be an improvement.

6.50 Providing different services in the same setting makes life easier for people, especially for vulnerable people such as people who are homeless or living in temporary accommodation, or the frail. It can also be the first step towards achieving greater integration between public services.

6.51 **The principle of co-location will therefore be included in the new national commissioning framework described in Chapter 7.**

6.52 We want to make co-location in purpose-built facilities easier. **To do this we will explore how the Government can support local authorities and PCTs in developing more effective partnerships to fund and develop joint capital projects.** We will work with the Office of the Deputy Prime Minister and other government departments to explore how we can combine or align funding scheme credits to increase the support these funds already provide to councils in developing innovative and community-based support. This work will link in with the new guidance on community hospitals and facilities.

Bromley-by-Bow healthy living centre – diverse services for a diverse community

The Bromley-by-Bow centre in Tower Hamlets is an excellent example of a centre providing a range of services, all co-located. People can see a GP and then have a healthy meal, get information about other services and sign up for a course or exercise programme all in one place. The services are well-used and popular.

Sabnam Ullah, 32, is a full-time mum from Bromley-by-Bow in East London. She's been attending the Healthy Lifestyle programme run at the Bromley-by-Bow healthy living centre for almost two years. Thanks to the programme leader, Krys, she's learnt lots of things she didn't know before and she's shared these with her mother and her sisters. Taking part in the programme has made a huge difference to the health of her entire family. She tells her story:

"I'd gained about a stone in weight after my younger son was born and I thought I'd go along to try to lose a few pounds. There's also a history of diabetes in my family so I wanted to reduce my weight and my risk. Diabetes is a big problem in the Bengali community because our diet is richer. It used to be just fish and vegetables, but now it's more meat-oriented. Also, people stay at home more here than they would in Bangladesh, so they're not walking around a lot and don't exercise much."

"Normally we eat our evening meal at 9pm after my husband has come home from work. We eat lots of rice, potatoes, nan or chappati. But with Krys we talked about eating less in the evening, cutting down on carbohydrates and eating more vegetables and fish instead. We also talked about the right foods to eat during Ramadan to stay healthy."

"I really enjoy the exercise; I'd never be able to go to a gym because I don't drive and it's so expensive to join. The centre's a really happy place; there are always people laughing and it's a great place to socialise."

6.53 Co-location does not have to happen by bringing in more services to the health setting – it can work the other way round. For instance, the 3,500 Sure Start children's centres that will be in place by 2010 will provide significant opportunities for improving the health of parents and young children under 5. They will provide:

- a means of delivering integrated, multi-agency services;
- a means of improving choice;
- a means of accessing hard-to-reach populations and therefore of reducing health inequalities;
- a means of delivering key components of the National Service Framework for Children, Young People and Maternity Services, such as the child health promotion programme;
- a means of achieving Choosing Health objectives (for example reducing smoking in pregnancy, increasing breastfeeding rates, improving diet and nutrition, reducing levels of childhood obesity, and promoting positive mental health and emotional well-being).

6.54 In the most disadvantaged areas, children's centres will be providing a range of integrated services, including family support, health information and integrated early education and childcare. In these areas we would expect to see more community health services for young children and parents being provided from children's centres. We will be encouraging PCTs and local authorities to plan the development of

centres and the delivery of integrated services together. As part of our monitoring of the performance of local authorities in improving children's outcomes in the early years, including using children's centres, we are likely to develop a list of performance indicators, which will include health outcomes. These outcomes in turn are likely to include performance indicators around child obesity, child mortality and teenage pregnancy.

6.55 Some children's centres are being developed from Sure Start local programmes currently led by PCTs. When new children's centres are developed on health sites, it will often make sense for PCTs to lead the children's centre. PCTs and local authorities should consider and agree such arrangements through children's trust arrangements.

Service reconfiguration
6.56 Overall, we are laying out a vision for the development of primary and community facilities. We intend to shift resources and activity from acute

Brighton and Hove

Through the Brighton and Hove Children's Trust, the local authority and the PCT have developed a model of health service delivery through the city's Children's Centres. Multi-disciplinary teams will comprise health visitors, midwives, family support staff and Playlink workers, as well as contributions from a dedicated speech and language therapist and possibly other specialist staff, depending on local need. Health professionals will make up the most significant element of these teams, which will greatly enhance the core service of each Children's Centre.

to local settings, in direct response to patient feedback.

6.57 It will be essential for commissioners to develop new facilities by linking decisions about primary and community facilities with decisions about acute provision. Commissioners need to reshape acute provision in line with this White Paper's strategy. **In particular, PCTs, SHAs and acute trusts will need to review their current plans for major capital procurement, to ensure that any such plans are compatible with a future in which resources and activity will move into primary and community settings. Positive endorsement of major capital** proposals will happen only where this compatibility clearly exists.

6.58 We encourage commissioners to use a Department of Health tool that is under development to support service reconfiguration. SHAPE (Strategic Health Asset Planning and Evaluation) is a web-enabled toolkit which is being designed to support the strategic planning of services and physical assets across a whole health economy. It takes as its starting point the current clinical activity, projections of need and potential demand, and the existing estate or physical capacity. SHAPE will provide a scenario-planning tool to determine an optimum service delivery model and to identify investment needs and disinvestment opportunities to support delivery of the model.

6.59 Service reconfigurations can be unnecessarily time-consuming, costly, and highly controversial. **So over the next few months we will review the process of statutory consultation and service reconfiguration, with a view to ensuring that local people are engaged from the outset in identifying opportunities, challenges and options for change. The need for change should be explained clearly and reconfiguration processes should be swift and effective. It is important that the local community feels a real sense of involvement in and ownership of the decision.** New guidance will be drawn up in discussion with stakeholders – including local authorities and PCTs, as well as patient and user groups – as a result of this review.

6.60 Finally, throughout this White Paper we have been clear that the focus on greater prevention, and on greater activity in primary and community settings, is crucial to delivering an NHS that is high quality, that focuses on health and well-being, and that is cost-effective in the medium term. Unless this White Paper strategy is pursued – and the consequent service reconfigurations take place – some local financial imbalances may never be corrected.

6.61 For the small minority of trusts in persistent deficit, we have recently supported local engagement of external 'turnaround teams' to diagnose problems and to recommend solutions. These teams currently only cover one group of organisations and localities needing performance improvement support through ISIP. As we consider ISIP plans and the challenges facing local areas going forward, we will refocus elements of ISIP. **So for local areas that are in persistent deficit, we will again facilitate the local engagement of external 'service reconfiguration' teams, to help tackle the root causes of local imbalances. This will happen later in 2006.**

Transport

6.62 Transport can be a barrier to accessing care. The Social Exclusion Unit estimates that 1.4 million people miss, turn down or simply choose not to seek health care because of transport problems.

6.63 The issue of how people will be able to get to services should be given greater prominence in decisions on the location of new health and social care facilities. PCTs and local authorities should be working together to ensure that new services are accessible by public transport.

6.64 Existing facilities should also work closely with accessibility planning partnerships (in those areas that produce local transport plans) to ensure that people are able to access health care facilities at a reasonable cost, in reasonable time and with reasonable ease.

6.65 Providing more care in community facilities should help to reduce transport problems (see the case study opposite). However, for care to be accessible to all, transport will still need to be available. Transport considerations will still be important for those who cannot walk to the local service, those who do not have access to their own vehicle, or those who have a medical need for non-emergency patient transport services.

6.66 Indeed, the public told us that transport to health and social care services was an issue that needed improvement. This message came particularly strongly from older people and from people in rural areas.

So many people in rural areas just do not access services because they don't have the transport.

PARTICIPANT AT THE CITIZENS' SUMMIT IN BIRMINGHAM

CASE STUDY

Local services reducing transport needs

If we have more services in the community this will increase convenience and reduce the need for travel. That is certainly the case for the citizens of **Birmingham**, as some kidney patients are now getting dialysis treatment at their local GP surgery. Instead of travelling miles to Heartlands Hospital three times a week, patients in Sutton Coldfield are now using Ashfurlong Medical Centre, in Tamworth Lane, right on their doorstep.

For 22-year-old Gemma Ford, the new dialysis unit has made a huge difference. She says "I started my dialysis at Heartlands Hospital in Birmingham, but it took 30–45 minutes to get there by car. Now that I go to Ashfurlong it only takes me 15 minutes." Gemma is also now able to do a full day at work because the unit stays open later and she has her dialysis at 5pm.

If successful, the pioneering scheme could even pave the way for other GP surgeries across the country to follow suit. The unit opened in January 2005 and has five dialysis machines treating up to 25 patients a week. The move by Heartlands Trust and Birmingham PCT comes as kidney and renal problems continue to soar in the city, particularly among ethnic minorities.

Gemma is now able to do a full day at work as a hairdresser.

6.67 To tackle this, we will extend eligibility for the patient transport service (PTS) to procedures that were traditionally provided in hospital, but are now available in a community setting. This will mean that people referred by a health care professional for treatment in a primary care setting, and who have a medical need for transport, will receive access to the PTS.

6.68 We will also extend eligibility for the hospital travel costs scheme (HTCS) to include people who are referred by a health care professional for treatment in a primary care setting, providing that they meet the existing low-income criteria.

6.69 We will work with the Healthcare Commission to provide national standards for what people can expect from patient transport services. **In addition, we will update finance guidance to reflect new arrangements and will develop reference costs for patient transport services. Finally, we will explore options for accrediting independent-sector providers of patient transport services, to ensure common minimum standards.**

6.70 While we have focused here on transport to NHS services, social care will not be neglected. The closer partnership between the NHS and local authorities will also encompass the provision of universal services, including transport. The needs of people accessing the services will also be considered, as part of the wider strategic needs assessments (including accessibility planning) that local authorities will be encouraged to undertake. In future, local authorities and PCTs will need to work together to influence providers of local transport in planning transport networks.

Incentives and commissioning

6.71 While undoubtedly powerful, a better evidence base from our demonstration programmes and a greater level of community facilities will not be enough on their own. In addition we will need to strengthen commissioning and tariff-setting.

6.72 Practices and PCTs, with their strengthened focus on commissioning, have the potential to drive the development of specialist care in the community, working closely with clinicians in secondary care and with their local social care colleagues.

6.73 Commissioning is discussed more fully in the next chapter. Payment by Results (PbR) creates incentives for providers to offer services in the most cost-effective manner.

6.74 To do this, at least three things need to happen. First, we need to make it possible to apply the tariff to activity in community settings. So measures of activity and appropriate case-mix classifications need to be specified for care delivered outside the hospital setting.

6.75 Second, and in parallel, tariffs for whole packages of care will need to be 'unbundled' in certain areas, to allow parts of the package to be provided in the community. This will mean that activities such as diagnostics or elements of rehabilitation are separated out and priced accordingly. The aim will be to develop PbR so that the tariff can be applied on the basis of the case mix, regardless of the type of provider or of whether care is delivered in an acute or a community setting. This means that the tariff will need to take account of such issues as fairness for different providers and adjustments for case-mix complexity, where applicable.

6.76 Third, the tariff needs to be based on the most cost-effective way of delivering a service. Currently it is based on the average cost of providing a service as reported by NHS trusts.

Over time, we will move tariffs to reflect best and most cost-effective practices. Where the activity is delivered at lower cost for the same clinical quality in the community, then tariffs would be expected to move towards these lower levels, allowing for any appropriate adjustments.

6.77 We will therefore:

- **introduce the flexibility to unbundle the tariff for diagnostics and post-acute care. We will initially focus on the conditions in the demonstrations specialties which make the most use of diagnostic services, and on those which are the key causes of bed-day use in the NHS and which have the potential to be delivered outside the hospital. We will introduce this in 2007/8;**
- **provide further flexibility to unbundle other services by the end of the decade at the latest;**
- **introduce appropriate data collections so that details of activity delivered in community-based settings and/or by new providers can be processed under PbR;**
- **start to apply the tariff to activity delivered in community-based alternatives to acute hospitals from 2007/08. We will focus initially on the key procedures in the demonstration specialties, especially those where costs may be lower in a community setting;**

- **increasingly seek to set tariff levels that represent truly cost-effective delivery – not just the average of all providers – across all activity, whether in an acute or a community setting. We will do this at the earliest possible opportunity.**[9]

6.78 We must also ensure that community-based specialist care is fully integrated into patient choice. PCTs can already include community-based alternatives to care on Choose and Book menus. We will develop the necessary information for people to make informed choices. **As a minimum people will have specialty-level-clinical quality data as well as timely patient experience data about specialist services in the community.**

6.79 **PCTs should also be implementing appropriate performance measures to ensure that the overall level of referrals to more specialist care is sustainable.** There are a number of ways to do this, such as benchmarking or the provision of referral guidelines, but PCTs will be best placed to determine what works best locally.

6.80 Shifting care closer to home is one of the pillars that supports our vision of improved community health and social care. What we are seeking is nothing less than a fundamental change in the way health and social care operates, a change that will inspire staff to deliver better quality care and that will put people in control. The next chapter sets out how we will ensure that this vision becomes a reality.

References

1   Derek Wanless, *Securing Our Future Health: Taking a Long Term View*, April 2002

2   Ham, York, Sutch and Shaw. *Hospital bed utilisation in the NHS – Kaiser Permanente and the US Medicare programme: analysis of routine data.* 2003

3   Hospital Episode Statistics 2004/05. Includes HRG codes H82–H89 capturing all neck or femur fractures

4   Chief Executive's Report to the NHS (page 8). December 2005

5   Situation Reports (Sitreps) – data collected by the Department of Health

6   Professor John Young. *A Multi-Centre Study of the Effectiveness of Community Hospitals in Providing Intermediate Care for Older People.* St Luke's Hospital, Bradford, 2005

7   Ham, York, Sutch and Shaw. *Hospital bed utilisation in the NHS – Kaiser Permanente and the US Medicare programme: analysis of routine data.* 2003

8   Meads, G. *Participate,* University of Warwick, 2004, referenced on www.developingcommunityhospitals.org.uk

9   More detail on these commitments will be given in the forthcoming publication *Framework for the future of PBR 2007/08 and beyond,* due in autumn 2006.

CHAPTER 7

Ensuring our reforms put people in control

Ensuring our reforms put people in control

This chapter on the structures in place for governance and empowerment includes:

- a stronger local voice to effect change in services when needed;
- the roles of local authorities and Primary Care Trusts (PCTs);
- a framework for commissioning;
- the benefits of Practice Based Commissioning (PBC);
- ensuring best value for money, through improved provision and commissioning of services;
- supporting social enterprise and the third sector.

Introduction

7.1 Previous chapters set out the public's priorities for reform – better health and well-being, convenient access to high-quality services, support for those with longer-term needs, and care in the most appropriate setting, closer to home. In order to ensure that these priorities are delivered, we need to put mechanisms in place that ensure the public's needs and wishes are acted upon.

7.2 The current changes to the health and social care system, as set out recently in *Health Reform in England* and *Independence, Well-being and Choice*, are designed to do just that:

- Choice means people will increasingly determine what services they want, and where. Providers that offer these services will thrive; those that do not won't.
- Individual budgets will put far more control in the hands of people who use social care services, affecting the way six different income streams can be spent around their personal needs. Markets will need to be developed to ensure that they have an appropriate range of services to choose from.
- PBC will put more control in the hands of primary care professionals, who develop care packages for their patients. PBC will give local practices much more scope to provide alternatives to specialist referral, treatment

and follow-up where appropriate, for example nurse-led clinics and follow-up telephone calls.
- Payment by Results (PBR) encourages practices and PCTs to commission care safely and more cost-effectively in the places people choose to be treated, encouraging shifts from inpatient to day case and outpatient, and treatment outside the secondary care sector.

7.3 This chapter explains how these reforms can be developed so that the system itself puts people first.

7.4 At the same time as giving people greater choice and control over the services they use, we also need to ensure that everyone in society has a voice that is heard. When people get involved and use their voice they can shape improvements in provision and contribute to greater fairness in service use.

Services that engage citizens and respond to their concerns

7.5 Systematically and rigorously finding out what people want and need from their services is a fundamental duty of both the commissioners and the providers of services. It is particularly important to reach out to those whose needs are greatest but whose voices are often least heard.

7.6 People's voices – their opinions, preferences and views – need to be heard at a local level as that is where the vast majority of spending decisions are taken and where key priorities are set. They need to be heard in a variety of different ways. And they have to count – at present, people do not feel that health and social care organisations listen enough to their views. It is important that these arrangements offer scope to groups – such as children and young people – who do not always have a choice to participate.

7.7 There is progress that we can build on. Some organisations in the NHS, local government and the voluntary, community and private sectors have engaged users and citizens in a systematic and robust way. However, these are not the norm. We want to see all parts of health and social care open and responsive to what people feel and prefer.

7.8 People's voices will be most effective if they directly affect how resources are used. Therefore, the forthcoming guidance on commissioning (see paragraph 7.51)

CASE STUDY

Networking to cope with HIV

When you are living with a life-threatening disease, such as HIV, you want to have as much say as possible in your treatment. To achieve this, Camden PCT established a sexual health clinic patients' network for people with HIV.

This network has helped people with HIV take responsibility in making healthier lifestyle and treatment choices by increasing patient involvement. Members of the network have been able to encourage and support each other.

A member of staff said: "We aimed to make sure that all HIV-positive patients were informed, consulted and able to have their say in the clinic in all areas relating to their physical and emotional well-being."

The network has succeeded in reaching out to under-represented minority groups – in particular, heterosexual female African patients and heterosexual couples. It has moved from being an advisory group to becoming a fully independent patient network, responsible for its own membership, recruitment and organisation. It has also become more involved in the clinic's decision-making process by sending representatives to monthly senior management meetings.

Finally, the network has made a major contribution to setting up a new in-house pharmacy and recruiting a part-time professional patient representative.

Taken from *Getting over the wall*, Department of Health, 2004

will set out how PCTs, practices and local authorities can ensure their decisions are fully informed and responsive. It will encourage PCTs and local authorities to consider the potential for Local Area Agreements (LAAs) to facilitate joint public engagement on health and social care.

7.9 As well as the increased focus on public engagement in commissioning, we also expect more rigorous fulfilment of existing duties to involve and consult the public in how services are provided. This applies to new providers too. Systematic engagement will complement other mechanisms already in place, such as Foundation Trust membership – which already involves half a million people – and patient surveys.

7.10 To assist organisations, advice and best practice guidance will come from the new Patient and Public Involvement resource centre, which will work closely with the Social Care Institute for Excellence (SCIE) and the Care Service Improvement Partnership (CSIP).

7.11 Organisations providing or commissioning NHS or local authority funded care must ensure local people play a full part in the planning, design and delivery of their services. How well they succeed will form part of their overall annual performance rating. Organisations will be expected to provide information on how they engage with the public.

7.12 In taking this forward, we intend to build on our experience since the *NHS Plan* in 2000. We will build on what works – there are lessons to be learned from Foundation Trust approaches, from the progress made by patients' forums, from what many non-executives on PCTs have done, from our own *Your health, your care, your say* consultation and from innovations such as the National Institute for Health and Clinical Excellence's (NICE's) citizens' councils.

7.13 We are clear that there has to be a means for the collective voice of people to be heard. The public should be able to take a view of health and social care in the round, though we recognise that the local arrangements may well differ between commissioners and providers given their different roles.

7.14 We can see many advantages to strengthening the involvement of the public in the work of the health Overview and Scrutiny Committees (OSCs) in local authorities. Before we can decide on that, however, more

needs to be done to map out on a whole-system basis how we can best embed a stronger local voice coherently at every level.

7.15 We are, therefore, committed to completing our existing fundamental review designed to strengthen the arrangements for ensuring a strong local voice in health and social care by April 2006.

7.16 One important area where we can strengthen links to communities at the most local level is by using individual ward councillors as advocates for the communities they are elected to represent. **We will consider options for a 'community call for action' where issues of concern to a community have not been resolved through other channels. We will explore ways of giving local councillors a particular role in the process.**

7.17 The views and experiences of people must also play an important part in the regulation and inspection of quality in health and social care delivery. We will bring forward legislation to merge the Healthcare Commission and Commission for Social Care Inspection (CSCI), detailing the functions of the single organisation, and we will make explicit the requirement for the full involvement of the public in its work. Between now and then both organisations will continue to strengthen their arrangements to involve people in their activities.

7.18 People also, quite rightly, want easy and effective ways of complaining when services have not been good enough. **To do this, we will develop by 2009 a comprehensive single complaints system across health and social care. It will focus on resolving complaints locally with a more personal and comprehensive approach to handling complaints.**

7.19 Handling of complaints should happen speedily and effectively. The merger of the two regulators provides us with the opportunity to review where best to place the independent review stage of a joined-up complaints procedure.

7.20 We must also ensure that people with concerns or who wish to complain have access to effective support. This is particularly important for people who find it difficult to make their views heard. To ensure people are supported, the Patient Advice and Liaison Service (PALS) will need to continue to develop its capacity. The Independent Complaints Advocacy Service (ICAS) has been strengthened and the new, improved service comes on stream in April 2006.

7.21 We will go further in giving people the power to demand changes where community services are unresponsive or resistant to their needs. As well as the independent user surveys referred to earlier, **we will ensure that, where a specified number or proportion of users petition the service provider for improvements, the provider will have to respond, within**

a specified time, explaining how they will improve the service or why they cannot do so. This will apply to local GP practices as well as other services commissioned or provided by the PCT. **To facilitate the better use of surveys, the Department of Health will review the survey programme, reporting by autumn this year.**

7.22 We will also specify other **'local triggers'** relating to public satisfaction and service quality, to which a PCT will be expected to respond if there is evidence that the public's needs are not being met. These include:

- indicators identifying inequalities in provision;
- Strategic Health Authority (SHA) assessments of PCTs; commissioning effectiveness; and
- the results of inspections by the Healthcare Commission.

7.23 The PCT will be expected to publish its response to these triggers and will have 12 months to make improvements and, if necessary, will be given support in doing so, for example, through the procurement waves outlined in Chapter 3 above. If, following this, problems remain – as evidenced by further surveys or other indicators – the PCT will be required to undertake a comprehensive, best-value tender of services from any willing provider to ensure that local needs are met.

7.24 We have explained why there is a clear need to develop new voice arrangements that are both stronger and also fit for purpose in the new

system. While we are clear about the key elements, we still need to work with stakeholders on the detail; this we will do over the next few months.

Effective commissioning

7.25 The main responsibility for developing services that improve health and well-being lies with local bodies: primary health care practices, PCTs and local authorities. They have a vital role in making sure public resources are used effectively to promote health and well-being and to support high-quality services. Good local commissioning will help local people keep well and stay independent, and will provide real choices for their populations.

7.26 Commissioning is the process whereby public resources are used effectively to meet the needs of local people. The voices of local people will be vitally important in improving this process. Public involvement is part of our wider strategy to facilitate high-quality commissioning and, in particular, to make joint commissioning a reality.

The role of local authorities
7.27 Across England, social services departments in local authorities are locally accountable for securing high-quality, responsive care services for their local residents. Increasingly, this requires them to lead and co-ordinate the activities of different service providers across the public, private and voluntary sectors in their community, designing services around the needs of people rather than those of the providers.

7.28 If individuals using services are to have real empowerment and choice, the market will need to be developed and supported to offer a wider range of services, tailored to meet the rising expectations and needs of an increasingly elderly, diverse and culturally rich population.

7.29 To do this services must be secured for the whole community, including for those people who will fund their own care. It means developing commissioning that stimulates and supports the local market. It means strengthening local community capacity through using the voluntary, community and independent sectors. And it means working closely with providers to develop strategic workforce plans as part of the support for local markets.

The role of PCTs
7.30 PCTs are now responsible for over 85 per cent of the NHS budget. Over the next two years, we will not only continue to increase NHS funding at an unprecedented rate, but we will also make that funding much fairer. Every part of the country will get more, but the communities in most need will get most. Resources are allocated to PCTs on the basis of need – known as the 'weighted capitation funding formula'. This ensures that all areas receive their fair share and areas with the greatest need receive the most funding. In 2003/04, the best-off areas were 30 per cent above their target funding levels, while the worst-off areas were 20 per cent below. We are correcting this imbalance. By 2007/08, the 5 per cent most needy PCTs will receive allocations of £1,710 per person. The allocation per head in spearhead PCTs will be £1,552 per person, and the national average will be £1,388 per person.

7.31 PCTs are responsible for improving health and well-being by securing the best possible care for their

Figure 7.1 Range of distance from target, 2003/04 to 2008/09

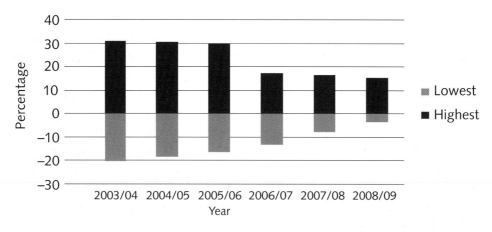

Source: Department of Health Finance

local residents within the 'fair shares' resources they have been allocated. They will discharge this responsibility by securing the best and most equitable primary health care for their community by devolving indicative budgets to practices, by holding practices to account and by working with them to redesign clinical pathways and ensure that services are provided as close to the community as possible. They will also secure other community services either by commissioning services from separate providers or by providing services directly themselves. In either case, both PCTs and practices will be responsible for achieving best value in meeting the needs of local people.

7.32 PCTs were established three years ago, covering 303 different areas. There are many examples in different parts of the country of how PCTs have already significantly improved services and secured better health outcomes. In order to build on these achievements, SHAs and PCTs were asked last year to consider whether they had the right structure for the challenges ahead, in particular understanding and meeting the needs of local communities in partnership with local authorities, while also securing the best services and value from acute hospitals.

7.33 In most parts of the country, consultations are now taking place on options for changing PCT boundaries. Many of the options provide for PCT boundaries to be the same as those of local authorities with social services

responsibilities, which would make it easier to achieve better integration of health and social care.

7.34 Decisions on PCT configurations will be made later this year, following local consultation. All PCTs, including those whose boundaries are unchanged, will then be expected to review their capability and 'fitness for purpose', looking especially at their skills in commissioning. This will be supported by a well-defined development and change-management programme.

7.35 Under the Civil Contingencies Act 2004, PCTs will retain the responsibility to contribute to multi-agency planning and response in the event of a major incident, whether accidental or intentional. All arrangements for the provision of community services will need to ensure that those services contribute to planning for, and are able to respond to, any major or catastrophic incident involving the PCT, including the provision of mutual aid to other organisations within the local health community.

Utilising existing flexibilities and reforms to improve our focus on health
7.36 Local authorities and PCTs already have significant flexibilities under the Health Act 1999 to develop integrated working, which allows a greater investment in prevention and health, for example through pooling budgets, transferring resources from health to local authority bodies or vice versa, and entering into lead commissioning arrangements. The *NHS*

Improvement Plan[1] envisaged that use of these flexibilities would become extensive in the next few years.

7.37 For children's services, joint commissioning by local authorities, PCTs, practice-based commissioners and other partners will be done through the Children's Trust. Joint commissioning strategies will be based on the *Children and Young People's Plan*, which is informed by children, young people, their families and the community.[2]

7.38 We will also continue to support the development of commissioning for adult social care and strengthen joint working via the development of the joint strategic needs assessment as set out in Chapter 2.

7.39 The Department of Health will sponsor work to develop and disseminate good-practice models of commissioning for people with long-term conditions/disabled people, within the partnership framework that the Department of Health has with the Disability Rights Commission. This work will assist PCTs to commission services for their whole communities, including excluded groups, and to reduce health inequalities through targeting people at highest risk of ill-health. It will help drive up standards of access for all health and social service users. The work will be developed with partners from health and social services and service users themselves.

CASE STUDY

Pooling budgets in Redbridge

The London Borough of Redbridge operates a £40 million Section 31 Agreement (Health Act 1999) covering services such as social work, health visiting, school nursing, speech and language therapy, child and adolescent mental health services, educational psychology and educational welfare services.

Pooling of budgets with the local PCT has smoothed the process of agreeing residential placements in particular, and has made supporting parent and children's visits less complicated. There is more clarity about the resources available to each partner and the respective priorities.

Partnership working has become easier as the pooled fund is seen as being available to the population of children who receive a service from this part of the Children's Trust. Partners are more worried about whether the needs of the child concerned meet general criteria for a service and are less worried about whether their needs are primarily health, social care or education related.

7.40 Shared use of an individual's records, with the individual's consent, will make it easier for different services to provide integrated care to the individual user, something that will become easier with the NHS electronic care record.

Practice Based Commissioning

7.41 Our health reforms are changing the way that health care is commissioned. As a result of PBR and patient choice, finance will flow to where clinical activity takes place. PBC reflects the fact that, every day, in the decisions they make, primary care professionals already commit NHS resources on behalf of PCTs as a matter of course.

7.42 Under PBC, health care practices will receive indicative budgets and will be able to see how much of their secondary care budget is going on, for example, emergency hospital admissions. They will then be able to free up money to do more for people with long-term conditions and other priority needs. PBC will provide incentives to avoid unnecessary stays in hospitals, which the public would prefer to avoid, and enable them to devote more resources to more cost-effective prevention, including social care.

7.43 PBC will give primary health care teams a real freedom and a real incentive to look after their population more effectively. It is the health equivalent of individual budgets in social care and will give primary care professionals control over resources.[3]

7.44 We also expect that PBC will lead to the development of more responsive and innovative models of joined-up support within communities. Some practices, such as Bromley-by-Bow practice in Tower Hamlets, are already successfully developing such services. We will ensure that practice-based commissioners are free to pursue similar innovations, for example through locally enhanced well-being services.

7.45 Indeed, we will encourage more joint commissioning between primary care and local authority teams in their local areas. And PBC should increase the creative use of Health Act 1999 flexibilities. **We will highlight good practice in using the flexibilities as part of future guidance on PBC.** We are also aware of the need to understand better the inter-relationship between local authority Fair Access to Care Services (FACS) eligibility criteria and PBC in the light of practical experience.

7.46 PCTs will hold health care practices accountable for their use of public money under PBC. PCTs will be expected to support practices that are innovative and entrepreneurial, working with them to redesign clinical pathways and secure the services that are needed locally (for example, ensuring that diagnostic services can be provided in a local health centre or community hospital for the patients of several practices, or expanding the provision of community nursing services to support people at home or exploring opportunities to develop complementary and alternative health therapies). But where health care practices are unwilling or unable to make good use of PBC, PCTs will need to provide appropriate challenge and support.

Information for commissioning

7.47 At every level, good commissioning depends upon good information. The *Choosing Health* public health information and intelligence strategy is developing information about communities that will help commissioners and providers target health improvement resources to those who will most benefit from them, or who are least able to engage with mainstream services. PCTs and local authorities will be better able to understand the health inequalities and challenges they face.

7.48 The Director of Adult Social Services and the Director of Public Health will carry out regular needs assessments of their local population. This will require analysis and interpretation of data held by PCTs, local authorities, youth offending teams, the police, independent providers, voluntary and community organisations, Supporting People, the Department for Work and Pensions, census data and other data sources. This will enable the establishment of a baseline of current population needs in order to effectively plan for the future and provide the information needed to stimulate and develop the social care market.

7.49 This will ensure that PCTs and local authorities have a better understanding of their local populations

and the challenges they face in tackling health inequalities. They should already be mapping and targeting at-risk populations as part of their community strategies and local Neighbourhood Renewal strategies (in areas receiving Neighbourhood Renewal funding).

7.50 This joint work on mapping can be strengthened by using tools such as Health Impact Assessments, and working across agencies on developing and responding to Health Equity Audits. *Choosing Health* set out our proposals to develop a tool to assess local health and well-being which will help PCTs and local authorities jointly to plan services and check on progress in reducing inequalities – a health and well-being equity audit. The Quality and Outcomes Framework (QOF) is now starting to provide useful data to inform and support effective commissioning.

Providing support through a national commissioning framework

7.51 In *Health Reform in England*, the Department of Health committed to publish during summer 2006 comprehensive guidance on commissioning health services – from PBC to national commissioning of specialist services.

7.52 This guidance will be the first stage of a comprehensive commissioning framework, setting out tools and approaches that lead to high-quality commissioning.

Mapping pinpoints diabetes in Slough

Action Diabetes was launched in Slough in October 2004, to raise awareness of Type 2 diabetes in areas with populations most at risk. The project was designed and implemented by Dr Foster with the support of Slough PCT. Together they targeted hard-to-reach groups using health needs mapping (HNM) analysis, in partnership with Experian. This targeted approach and the use of volunteers from the local community meant that people were advised on lifestyle changes before their condition worsened. Interim results showed that the four-week campaign produced a 164 per cent increase in diabetes referrals among the most at-risk communities.

Grace Vanterpool, Diabetes Clinical Lead, Slough PCT, found this an invaluable technique for identifying at-risk groups:

"By using HNM we've been able to calculate where the highest concentration of undiagnosed sufferers are, and implement a local marketing campaign to target these groups. This campaign has finally given me the opportunity to engage with local communities on a larger and far more effective scale, mainly because of the local volunteers. Awareness levels seem to be greater than ever before."

Zishan Shafi, a volunteer health counsellor for the programme, really enjoyed the experience. "As I'm young, I can go into colleges and people will listen. I've even made progress sat at the mosque, giving out materials and explaining the dangers. My sister has diabetes and she's been coming with me to talk about her experiences – it really helps."

7.53 We commit to producing two further parts of this framework by the end of 2006. First, following consultation on *Independence, Well-being and Choice*, we will develop guidance on joint commissioning for health and well-being. This guidance will recommend what healthy living and well-being services are most effective or promising. Local commissioners will be able to use it as an assessment tool as they jointly undertake regular strategic reviews of health and well-being needs, and then specify and commission services.

7.54 It will also detail how those involved in different levels of commissioning can work together to improve market management and facilitate a shift towards preventative services.

7.55 Second, we will develop commissioning guidance specifically for those with ongoing needs by the end of 2006. This is necessary because commissioning for people with long-term needs has too often been episodic and organisational, rather than focused on individuals. Joint commissioning in this area is crucial, because 80 per cent of those using social care also have a long-term health care need.

7.56 The commissioning framework will also consider contracting for services. The Department of Health's summer 2006 guidance for NHS commissioners will include a model contract for hospital services.

7.57 A key theme of the overall commissioning framework will be to encourage commissioners to use open tendering as a way of ensuring innovation, quality and value from any willing provider so as to improve quality and offer real choice to people who use services. This will be important to secure the participation of the independent and voluntary sectors, especially in areas experiencing health inequalities or where there is inequality in accessing services.

Supporting best practice

7.58 The NHS has taken great steps to deliver benefits from investment and reform through the development of an Integrated Service Improvement Programme (ISIP) in each local health community of PCTs, SHAs, trusts and practices. The ISIP considers how patient and user needs can be addressed through clinical service redesign based on world-class best practice culled from the Modernisation Agency and NHS Institute for Innovation and Improvement.

7.59 The programme also considers how these developments are supported by IT changes from NHS Connecting for Health and workforce reform on areas such as dealing with long-term conditions and urgent care. The programme is assured by the Office for Government Commerce and supports effective commissioning and local delivery planning. The ISIP will adapt, with closer integration with CSIP, to support joint planning and commissioning with local authorities.

Assessing commissioning

7.60 Finally, we will make commissioning more important in performance assessment. Working with SHAs, the Healthcare Commission and CSCI, the Department of Health will develop during 2006 a revised assessment for PCTs and local authorities to focus more effectively on how well they are discharging their commissioner functions, separately and jointly. This will build on the PCT diagnostic development programme being piloted in 2006. CSCI and the Healthcare Commission will inspect local commissioners to ensure joint commissioning becomes a major part of commissioning work.

7.61 The present performance assessment regime, for PCTs in particular, is overly focused on provider output measures, such as the number of patients breaching hospital access maximum waits. The new regime will focus more broadly on how well PCTs succeed in meeting the health needs and expectations of their populations.

7.62 Ultimately, for truly effective joint commissioning to occur, the performance management and assessment systems of health and social care need to be aligned. Having different performance measures and targets for PCTs and local authorities has not facilitated joint commissioning.

7.63 By 2008, we will ensure that both performance management systems are synchronised and that they clearly encourage good joint commissioning. This performance

management system will develop incentives for carrying out good joint commissioning and sanctions for failing commissioners.

Commissioning responsive services

7.64 Intrinsic to being a good commissioner is keeping under regular and systematic review the quality of those services that are commissioned on behalf of others. Local people need to be able to rely on this as one way of assuring quality. We need to support commissioners to do this well.

Strengthening social care provision

7.65 In some areas, local authorities are faced with weak and fragile social care and social services providers. This can be a consequence of the size of the local authority and associated market, differences in commissioning skills and competencies, or a lack of long-term, co-ordinated, strategic procurement of services. The result, however, is that local authorities can end up with poor value for money.

7.66 This weakness has a direct impact on the commissioning choices that local authorities can make. The fact that over 150 local social services departments are trying to commission services in isolation leads to weak procurement practices, including too many short-term contracts which hinder providers from making the longer-term investments that are required to raise service quality.

CASE STUDY

Connected Care in Hartlepool

People living in the poorest neighbourhoods with the greatest needs are often the least likely to have access to the services and support which would help them improve their lives and life chances. Connected Care is a pilot programme that aims to tackle this. It's being developed through a partnership between Turning Point, a charity providing services for people with complex needs, Hartlepool PCT, the local authority and a range of community groups, involving the local community in the design and delivery of services.

Alison Wilson, Director of Primary Care Development and Modernisation at Hartlepool PCT, describes how a recently completed audit is giving the Connected Care partners insights into how better connected services could improve the lives of those in the greatest need.

"For instance, someone with substance issues or learning difficulties would often get a raw deal in the past because they wouldn't know how to navigate through the system. Connected Care workers will be trained to understand what the different organisations offer so that if someone comes to them with housing issues they may also have problems with debt and with their health. Historically, they usually get one part of their problem dealt with or looked after but they tend to get pushed from pillar to post. This way they should see someone who has an overview of the whole system and can help with all their needs and complex issues."

7.67 There is, therefore, a pressing need, identified by the Gershon review,[4] to deliver greater standardisation through procurement and contracting in order to reduce bureaucratic costs to both commissioners and providers.

7.68 The Government has established Regional Centres of Excellence to support local authorities in delivering on the National Procurement Strategy for Local Government and in meeting their Gershon efficiency targets. This will also allow for benchmarking of services commissioned by individual local authorities across each region.

7.69 We believe that it is also necessary for local authorities to have a national organisation working with them to help them develop the market opportunities that they can work with.

7.70 We will ensure that CSIP, with support from the Department of Health, continues to work with local government to develop better the various social care markets so that social care users across the country have the benefit of a full range of social care services. We will also support this by delivering a procurement model and best practice guidance to underpin key aspects of our joint commissioning framework for health and well-being. This best practice will be driven further through health and social care as part of the ISIP in every health community.

Strengthening community health provision

7.71 Most PCTs provide community health services themselves. PCTs employ about 250,000 staff directly, including district and community nurses, health visitors, speech and language therapists and physiotherapists. These staff are involved in providing care to patients in partnership with GPs and hospitals, and in improving the well-being of communities and the people who live in them by providing advice, support and services which help people stay well or maximise their independence. Much of this work is done jointly with local government, which also has responsibilities for ensuring communities are healthy. There is no requirement or timetable for PCTs to divest themselves of provision.

7.72 A key priority for these staff is reducing health inequalities and promoting health. It is only through early interventions and a greater focus on prevention and public health that

Innovation by the seaside

Drug and alcohol misusers often find it very difficult to get the help they need. Southend-on-Sea PCT recognised this and established a new general practice – the Victoria Surgery – to meet their needs. A team including a specialist GP, nurse practitioner, two specialist community psychiatric nurses and skilled reception staff work at the practice.

In addition to normal opening hours, the Victoria Surgery is open two evenings a week between the hours of 6.30pm and 10.00pm, as this was felt to suit people with substance misuse problems. The practice's list size has grown to 658 patients.

Cathy Harlett is one of the community psychiatric nurses based at the Victoria Surgery.

"The care we offer is holistic, looking at lifestyle changes and harm minimisation," says Cathy. "Substance misuse is a big problem in this area and these patients find it difficult to fit in with normal GP practices. As well as receiving treatment for their substance or alcohol misuse, patients' health

is monitored so that any problems can be treated immediately. We also undertake normal routine procedures, which have often been neglected."

Twenty-nine-year-old 'J' is a patient at the Victoria Surgery, who has problems with substance misuse and epilepsy.

"I've been to another clinic, but this one works better for me. It's open for longer and you can drop in for a chat any time. It's good to have that kind of support. They help me with my epilepsy and they help people come off drugs. Coming here has definitely helped."

inequalities and the future burden of ill-health will be reduced.

7.73 Community staff are, therefore, especially well-placed to help take forward the strategic shift set out in

this White Paper. The changes we propose offer them new opportunities to develop their roles and to lead the process of shifting the focus towards prevention and public health, better integration of health and social care, and putting individuals and communities in greater control.

7.74 The local NHS also draws on the expertise of many other community health care providers. Most practices are run by GPs who are self-employed contractors. These GP practices are run as small businesses and employ salaried staff, mostly nurses, allied health professionals, managers and administrative staff.[5] A significant proportion of GPs are salaried staff, employed directly by their PCT or by a practice. All, quite rightly, are regarded as an integral part of the NHS.

7.75 Some pharmacists are self-employed people running their own business and employing other staff, while many work for pharmacy businesses ranging from single independents to large multiples. They, and other parts of the private sector, are playing an important part in the NHS. Some other services, including sexual health services, are often provided by the voluntary sector. Most mental health services are provided by specialist mental health trusts and PCTs, often integrating community and acute provision across social care and health. Voluntary and private sector providers also play a significant role, including in specialised services.

7.76 There is a plurality of providers in primary and community services, from the public, private and voluntary sectors. What matters most to the users of services is not who provides them, but how good the service is. We want

to build on the strengths of the current system. As the introduction of PBC gives primary health care providers greater control over the use of local funding, they will need to work with the full range of staff in primary and community services to agree with PCTs how these services can be enhanced.

Ensuring that services are responsive

7.77 The core responsibility of PCTs is to ensure that all services for patients continually improve, whether commissioned by practice-based commissioners, the PCT itself or jointly with local government, and whether provided by the PCT or another provider.

7.78 From 2007 and as part of the normal commissioning process, we will expect each PCT to develop a systematic programme to review the services it commissions on behalf of the local population, working with practice-based commissioners and other local partners.

7.79 PCTs will be expected to ensure that providers of community health services accord with the direction set out in this White Paper:

- Equity – Are services fair? Do they focus on the most vulnerable and those in the greatest need?
- Quality – Are patients satisfied with services? Are services designed around people's lives, putting individuals at the centre of all they do? Are services strongly geared towards preventing illness and promoting well-being? Do

they work seamlessly with services provided by other local partners?

- Value for money – Do services make the best possible use of taxpayers' money? Are they providing cost-effective care?

7.80 Priority for review should be given to services where there is public or local authority OSC concern, a high level of complaints or where locally agreed business plans are not being met.

7.81 PCTs will be expected to seek the views of patients and users as an integral part of this process. Annual surveys, independently conducted, to cover all primary and community health services (including GP practices – see Chapter 3) will play an important role, helping to ensure users feed back their views on the responsiveness and appropriateness of local services.

7.82 PCTs will also be expected to use benchmarking information to assess the performance of services against good practice and develop an improvement plan as part of their wider development programme where needed. We will work with PCTs, SHAs and other stakeholders to ensure that this benchmarking information is made available.

7.83 Where local reviews show that services are high quality, PCTs can continue with the existing provider – in many instances this will be the PCT itself.

7.84 PCTs may also decide to look for new ways of providing services following a service review, or as they seek to continuously improve patient care. PCTs may decide that new models of service provision can offer real opportunities that are good for patients and are supported by staff.

CASE STUDY

Unleashing public sector entrepreneurship

East Elmbridge and Mid Surrey Primary Care Trust has announced that it is continuing to move forwards with plans to put nurses and therapists in the driving seat by supporting further work to create a patient-focused, not-for-profit company to deliver nursing and therapy services to the PCT.

The company will be co-owned by the 700 employees currently working for the PCT across nursing and therapy disciplines, and will use established primary care contracting routes (specialist personal medical services) to provide NHS services (similar to contracts used by GPs). Central Surrey Health will use a social enterprise model with a focus on investing in the local community and adding ongoing value.

7.85 We expect PCTs to be robust in their management of services that do not deliver the necessary quality. Where there are deficiencies in service quality, PCTs will be required to set out a clear improvement plan as part of their wider development programme. This may include tendering for the service where standards fall below those expected, either immediately or where improvement goals are not delivered after one year.

7.86 Depending on the precise service to be provided, new providers could include GPs, nurse practitioners or pharmacists wanting to establish or expand services, a care trust, a social enterprise (which could be owned by staff on a co-operative basis), or a voluntary or private sector organisation.

7.87 If PCTs propose changes in the ownership of provision of their community services, staff will be fully and formally consulted before decisions concerning the future of provision are taken. We will work with our partners to explore what more could be done to give staff greater assurance on pension arrangements if they transfer to new enterprises delivering NHS services.

7.88 We have agreed to set up a working group to look at all of the workforce issues arising from this White Paper. The working group will include representation from the NHS and social care, trade unions and professional bodies.

7.89 PCT Boards will need to assure themselves and others that decisions about provision are made in the public interest. They will, therefore, need to develop mechanisms to deal with potential conflicts of interest, for example decisions about whether PCT provision should continue or whether alternative providers should be sought. Non-executives will have a key role in ensuring that the needs of all sections of the community are properly considered, that there is an evidence base for decisions and that these are made in a fair and transparent way.

7.90 Where PCTs provide services, as the majority now do, they will need to put in place clear governance procedures which ensure that there is no undue influence of the provider side on commissioning decisions. These procedures will include independent scrutiny by the SHA and will be transparent to all potential contractors and to staff.

7.91 PCTs will need to give a clear account of their actions, reporting progress in their annual report as part of an increased drive for public accountability. PCTs will also need to give account of their actions to the OSC of the local authority, which will be able to refer a PCT to the SHA if it believes the PCT is not discharging its responsibilities properly. OSCs will also be able to initiate their own review of a particular service.

Voluntary organisations should be included. In my community
Age Concern provides services for local people.

PARTICIPANT AT THE CITIZENS' SUMMIT IN BIRMINGHAM

7.92 We will develop and consult on more detailed guidance on all these issues during 2006.

Supporting the development of the third sector and social enterprise

7.93 One way of introducing high-quality provision will be to promote better use of health and social care 'third-sector' providers. They include organisations from the voluntary and community sector, as well as other forms of values-driven organisations such as co-operatives.

7.94 Such third-sector organisations can have advantages over the public sector in terms of better relations with particular groups (for instance mental health charities) or expert knowledge in a specific area (for instance single-disease bodies such as Diabetes UK) or expertise in a type of care (for instance voluntary hospitals).

7.95 We have established the Third Sector Commissioning Task Force, which includes representatives of the community and voluntary sector, social services, PCTs, Office of the Deputy Prime Minister, Home Office, Department for Education and Skills and the Department of Health, to address the key barriers to a sound commercial relationship between the public and the third sector. The task force will promote equality of access for third-sector providers alongside other sectors in the provision of public sector health and social care services.

7.96 The third sector, together with the private sector, already provides over 70 per cent of social care. However, there are currently considerable barriers to entry for the third sector in providing NHS services. If we are to utilise the expertise of third-sector providers, we need to lower these barriers.

CASE STUDY

Social enterprise in city academies

The creation of city academies has huge potential to create a school environment where health is central, not an add-on. The new city academy opening in Enfield in September 2007 recognises the need to help teenagers both live healthy lives and use health services.

Sponsored by the Oasis Trust, a faith-based social enterprise that brings together services for local communities, the academy will have a healthy living centre on site. The centre will have GPs, physiotherapy, counselling and other services accessible to students and the wider community. It is also expected to include a Children's Centre and a community café.

Healthy eating will also feature in the dining hall and on the curriculum. Pupils will be able to eat nutritious, locally grown, organic school meals. The school will also offer a foundation course for future nurses.

7.97 Currently, a range of issues including pensions and IT make it difficult for the third sector to compete on a level playing field. **We commit to look at how to tackle these issues and report later this year.**

7.98 As well as tackling the barriers to third-sector provision in this way, we also recognise that other proposals in this White Paper will affect the third sector, and we commit to involve and consult them as the detail of specific proposals are developed further and implemented.

7.99 There is also significant potential to support and encourage social enterprise from within the third sector, the public sector (including the NHS and local government) and the private sector. The social enterprise model uses business disciplines for social objectives, and re-invests profits to support them.

7.100 We will establish a Social Enterprise Unit within the Department of Health to co-ordinate our policy on social enterprise including third-sector providers and ensure that a network of support is put in place to encourage the wider use of social enterprise models in health and social care.

7.101 The Department of Health will also establish a fund from April 2007 to provide advice to social entrepreneurs who want to develop new models to deliver health and social care services. This fund will also address the problems of start-up, as well as current barriers to entry around access to finance, risk and skills, to develop viable business models. The Department of Health will tender for an organisation to run the fund and provide these services.

7.102 The options will be described in detail in the forthcoming publication on integrated provision described in *Health Reform in England*.

References

1   *NHS Improvement Plan: Putting People at the Heart of Public Services* (Cm 6268), The Stationery Office, June 2004

2   Further information on joint planning and commissioning of children and young people's services and maternity services is available at www.everychildmatters.gov.uk/strategy/planningandcommissioning

3   For further information see *Practice Based Commissioning Guidance 2006/07*, Department of Health, 2006, www.dh.gov.uk/practicebasedcommissioning

4   *Releasing resources to the front line: Independent review of public sector efficiency*, Sir Peter Gershon, HM Treasury, July 2004

5   A GP's income depends upon the practice profits, not an NHS salary (as with hospital consultants)

CHAPTER 8

Making sure change happens

Making sure change happens

This chapter on the mechanisms required for change includes:

- better information to support more joined-up services;
- how quality will be assured;
- mechanisms for a more joined-up service with health and social care colleagues working together;
- how the workforce must evolve to meet the needs of a changing service.

You should get a booklet that tells you the services that are available; no-one knows what there is. It takes a long time to get information on health or social care services as people don't know where to look for it.

PARTICIPANT AT THE CITIZENS' SUMMIT IN BIRMINGHAM

Introduction

8.1 To make sure change happens, we need high-quality information to help people choose and access services. The quality of the services people use must be guaranteed. And the health and social care workforce must develop to truly put people in control.

High-quality information

8.2 The need for high-quality information about people's conditions and the services available to them was highlighted as a central theme of the *Your health, your care, your say* listening exercise. Fifty-eight per cent of people who completed the online questionnaire thought that being given more information would give them more control over their health and well-being.

8.3 Without good information, people may access the wrong services or get to the right services too late – resulting in unnecessary discomfort and added complications. We know that over half the patients who attend Accident and Emergency (A&E) departments with minor ailments do so because they are not aware of alternative, possibly more convenient and cost-effective, services within their local community.

8.4 Earlier chapters have covered some information initiatives – most notably the information prescription in Chapter 5. However, this chapter looks at an overarching approach to making information accessible.

8.5 Most information that people require is already available. For instance, good information sources exist such as the NHS website (www.nhs.uk), which has a facility listing doctors, opticians, pharmacists and dentists searchable via postcode, and the Directgov website (www.direct.gov.uk), which now provides access to information on all local authority services.

8.6 However, sources such as the internet are not accessible to all. People told us in the listening exercise that their preferred means of getting information is face-to-face. Some local authorities and Primary Care Trusts (PCTs) have developed examples of good practice in making information available.

8.7 Yet not everybody has such easy access to information. We need an integrated approach to information that starts from the perspective of what people want.

8.8 During 2006, the Department of Health will review the provision of health and social care information to ensure that people who use those services have the information they need, when they need it, and in a wide variety of formats. We will do

Welcome centre in Manchester

When you are new to an area, it can be hard to get information on public services, especially if English isn't your first language. Based in Trinity Church, Cheetham and Crumpsall Welcome Centre in Manchester is a resource centre with a wealth of information for its diverse community.

Angela Kenney is a health visitor and was one of the driving forces behind the establishment of the centre, which opened in November 2004:

"We want anyone who walks into the centre to feel really welcome. Well over 30 languages are spoken around here and we greet visitors in their own language. Many people who are new to the area are refugees and asylum seekers but there are also people who have lived locally for several years and are still isolated.

"People can find out about benefits, find support on parenting issues, get help to access health services and other health information, learn how to get their children into school, sort out housing problems and get employment advice. We have a play area with a play development worker provided by Sure Start, and there are activities for the older children in the holidays. All the expertise is here, on the spot, in a relaxed café-style environment and there's a thriving 15-strong volunteer force, some of whom are in their eighties.

"It's a true partnership arrangement; the advisers here have a wealth of knowledge

and this has a knock-on effect for all of us as we become more aware of each other's roles."

For some visitors, the centre has been a real lifeline. Sinita Kaur, who has a son and a daughter, has lived in the area for many years:

"I heard about the centre from my health visitor and one of the workers here. My family was having a hard time because we were getting racist abuse and my children were frightened. Coming here gave me lots of support at a difficult time and I made loads of new friends. The advice worker was really helpful; she helped us to get re-housed and now life is so much better. My husband talked to the employment adviser and now he's in work.

"Everyone is so friendly and you can get everything sorted out in one place. The children love coming, they use the play area and there's always something to do. I've made friends and I love coming here every week."

this in partnership with people who use health and social care and their representative organisations, and we will also consider methods of helping people navigate round the many different services.

Integrating information

8.9 A starting point for this review will be that people have told us that sources of information on health and local authority services are not linked. People want information to meet their needs as individuals, not to be provided according to organisational boundaries.

8.10 To find the best way to do this, **we will pilot in 2006 a project involving a local authority and a PCT to develop an integrated approach to information**, leading to the development of a service specification and timetable for implementation. Our ambition is for PCTs and local authorities to jointly maintain an accessible database of all services and support groups in their local area.

8.11 We will also develop a specification for easily searching available information, by looking at existing models such as ChildcareLink.[1] To help local authorities and PCTs implement this commitment in a way that dovetails with the Government's broader eGovernment objectives, and to support individuals, families, carers and professionals providing advice, we will seek to design and implement a support application for social care needs.

The vision for 'SocialCareLink' will be to develop an application which enables individuals, families or carers to: navigate round the many different services, research providers and current service availability; access relevant reports; and email enquiries or requests to providers from one place.

People's own information

8.12 At the national Citizens' Summit, one of the areas that some people supported was for patients to have smartcards with their own medical records on them. These records could then be accessible wherever someone accessed services.

8.13 We are not persuaded that such cards are necessary. The NHS Connecting for Health strategy is already developing a system of electronic care records that will be accessible across the NHS by 2008. There are plans for these records to be accessible to social services from 2010. This key underpinning reform will avoid the need for people to repeat information about their condition, a major complaint in the listening exercise.

8.14 Having smartcards would require new technology to read the information contained on the card and there would also be occasions when people did not have the card with them when they needed treatment. Our existing approach offers more flexibility.

No objections to that [sharing information]. It was very frustrating saying the same thing over and over to different people.

RESPONDENT TO *INDEPENDENCE, WELL-BEING AND CHOICE*

CASE STUDY

Leicestershire CareOnline is a window on the world

Since it started in 2001 Leicestershire CareOnline (www.leicscareonline.org.uk) has been providing people with an easy-to-use website designed to meet the needs of disabled people, older people and carers, giving them access to a wide range of information relevant to their needs. It is part of Leicestershire County Council Social Services' 'Better Access to Better Services' initiative and is supported by the Leicestershire Partnership, which includes district councils, Leicester City Council, PCTs and charities representing people with disabilities, older people and carers.

The CareOnline team firmly believes that with the right support, the internet can help tackle loneliness, isolation and social exclusion, and to that end they train older

people and people with disabilities on a one-to-one basis in their own homes. This gives them more confidence in using computers and the internet and this can transform their lives. As one service user said: "this service has provided me with a window on the world".

Guaranteeing quality

8.15 The NHS has one of the strongest and most transparent systems for quality in the world: clear national standards, strong local clinical governance arrangements (to assure and improve quality locally), robust inspections and rigorous patient safety arrangements. The development of National Service Frameworks has helped to spread best practice in tackling specific conditions and caring for particular groups of people.

8.16 Social care quality is currently monitored by: the Commission for Social Care Inspection (CSCI) – the regulatory body for social care with additional powers to take an industry-wide view of social care; a set of statutory regulations and underpinning national minimum standards; and the General Social Care Council (GSCC) to regulate the social care workforce. CSCI will be merged with the Healthcare Commission to form a single regulatory body for health and social care, as referred to in Chapter 2.

Assessment of quality

8.17 We will ensure that our means of guaranteeing quality improve further, to reflect the changes in this White Paper. Chapter 6 sets out our desire to provide more specialised services in community settings. Presently, while the Healthcare Commission assesses hospitals and other specialist health providers, there are no recognised schemes of assessment for the provision of these services in the community.

8.18 We therefore propose to introduce a national scheme of accreditation for the provision of specialist care in the community, to apply to new entrants and existing providers. This will ensure that both services and the staff working there, such as practitioners with special interests, are working to safe, high-quality standards. We will discuss further with the Healthcare Commission, the Royal College of General Practitioners and other interested parties the best means of doing this.

8.19 We will also consider the wider need for assessment of the quality of primary care practices and other primary care providers. We will work with the Healthcare Commission to develop an appropriate scheme. This may well involve the Healthcare Commission in assessing and approving the professions' own accreditation schemes, where it believes these: provide a strong framework for service improvement, including holding to account poorer providers; are effective but non-bureaucratic; and meet the Commission's move towards more risk-based regulation.

8.20 For example, the Royal College of General Practitioners' Quality Team Development (QTD) scheme has already been used by some PCTs and over 2,000 practices to review their own performance. QTD is a framework to enable primary care teams and their PCTs to assess the quality of the services they provide for patients. Its focus is on the whole team, their functioning and the services they provide, and it meets the Healthcare Commission's requirements.

8.21 In social care, CSCI already regularly assesses all providers. The Department of Health, working closely with CSCI, is currently reviewing the existing national minimum standards established under the Care Standards Act 2000 and the associated regulations, to ensure a targeted and proportionate system of regulation, with a focus on dignity, quality and the best possible outcomes for people who use social care services.

8.22 In addition, all local councils are assessed annually and are required to produce a delivery and improvement statement to show how they are progressing against national objectives and targets.

8.23 Individual professionals in health and social care are also likely to participate in a regular reassessment of their fitness to practice. In the medical profession, proposals were developed by the General Medical Council following a consultation in 2000[2] but were put on hold following the fifth report of the Shipman Inquiry.[3] The Chief Medical Officer will shortly be advising the Government on the way forward, following a review of revalidation and other aspects of the regulation of doctors. A similar review of non-medical regulation has been carried out by the Department of Health and the result of that review will be published in the spring.

8.24 The Department for Education and Skills, in partnership with the Department of Health, will shortly introduce legislation to create a new vetting and barring scheme, as recommended in the Bichard Inquiry,[4] to tighten up procedures to prevent unsuitable people from gaining access to children or vulnerable adults through their work, whether paid or unpaid. The new scheme will build on the existing pre-employment checks available through the Criminal Records Bureau, the Protection of Vulnerable Adults scheme, the Protection of Children Act scheme and List 99. It will extend the coverage of the existing barring schemes and draw on wider sources of information, providing a more comprehensive and consistent measure of protection for vulnerable groups.

Regulation

8.25 Regulation will become more streamlined and joined up, following the publication of the *Wider Review of Regulation* in 2006. In *Health Reform in England*, we promised to publish a document on the role of regulation within the context of revised arrangements for performance management in summer 2006.

8.26 The NHS reform rules for 2007 and 2008 will then set out how performance measures, including Public Service Agreements, developmental standards and Local Development Plan priorities, can better be integrated and streamlined to reflect these principles, and to reflect the new, stronger focus on prevention and well-being.

8.27 The GSCC and its devolved counterparts have a duty to develop codes of practice and they have worked together in developing these codes as part of their contribution to raising standards in social care services

8.28 Comprehensive arrangements to improve quality, including better commissioning, national standards, best practice, and inspection were set out in *A First Class Service*.[5] These have been very successful in driving the improvements in quality set out in *Health Reform in England*.

For me, the perfect social worker would be a caring person and understand the needs of the service user and follow them through with all the provisions and adaptations or whatever it is. They should go back to the service user and find out whether the service user is happy with what he or she has done so far.

RESPONDENT TO *INDEPENDENCE, WELL-BEING AND CHOICE*

Patient safety

8.29 For people, the clinical outcome of care – whether they get better, whether the complications of their illness are minimised, whether their health is maintained in the long term – matters greatly. So too does ensuring that they are not inadvertently harmed in the process of care.

8.30 For these reasons, we will continue to give a high priority to clinical governance and patient safety. The programme of patient safety launched by the Chief Medical Officer's report *An organisation with a memory*[6] is becoming integral to local services.

8.31 But there is more to do. It is important that the reporting of adverse events and near misses through the National Patient Safety Agency's national reporting and learning system is fully extended into primary care and other out-of-hospital settings.

8.32 Worldwide most of the focus on patient safety has been within hospitals. The NHS has a unique opportunity to lead the world on developing reporting and learning for adverse events outside hospital so that safety can be improved and risks can be reduced for potentially hundreds of thousands of NHS patients over the years ahead.

Developing the workforce

8.33 The health and social care workforce is a huge army for good. There are now 1.3 million NHS staff engaging in hundreds of millions of contacts with patients each year, employed by over 10,000 practices, trusts and PCTs. There are 1.5 million employees in social care, with over 25,000 employers, providing a service to around 1.7 million adults at any one time.

8.34 This White Paper will mean changes for all staff, whether they are focusing more on prevention or working in new settings. These changes will be managed sensitively, made in full consultation with the staff involved and always with the interests of patients and professionals at their heart.

Working across boundaries

8.35 One fundamental change will be better integration between those working in the NHS and those working in social care. A better-integrated workforce – designed around the needs of people who use services and supported by common education frameworks, information systems, career frameworks and rewards – can deliver more personalised care, more effectively.

8.36 Key to closer integration will be joint service and workforce planning. The NHS and local authorities need to integrate workforce planning into

corporate and service planning. The Department of Health will consider and develop plans to achieve this in line with proposals to align service and budgetary planning across health and social care and in consultation with stakeholders. Workforce issues will also be fully integrated in service improvement planning by the Care Services Improvement Partnership and the NHS Integrated Service Improvement Programme (ISIP).

8.37 Integrating planning will facilitate joint working on the ground. The NHS Large-scale Workforce Change programme and the Skills for Care New Types of Worker pilots are providing significant learning to develop team-working across traditional agency boundaries. This will be complemented by the Partnerships for Older People projects developing prevention and well-being pilots that cut across the boundaries between health, social care, housing, benefits and other local services.

8.38 New health and social care multi-skilled teams will also be established to support people with ongoing needs (see Chapter 5). Underpinning the development of these teams will be common national competencies and occupational standards.

8.39 Increasingly, employers will plan around competence rather than staff group or profession. To encourage integration, we will bring skill development frameworks together and create career pathways across health

and social care. Staff will increasingly be expected to have the skills to operate confidently in a multi-agency environment, using common tools and processes.

8.40 Skills for Care and Skills for Health, in partnership with other relevant organisations, will together lead this work so that staff can develop skills that are portable, based on shared values, recognised across the sectors and built around the needs of patients and service users.

Putting people in control
8.41 A further major change will be the shift to put people in control of their care. Professionals will work to support and empower people to make their own decisions, wherever possible.

8.42 Individuals, their families and other carers need to understand the services that are available in order to make good choices, and they need to receive maximum support in obtaining their chosen service – wherever it is provided. **We will develop competencies for workers specifically trained to help individuals with health or social care needs to 'navigate' their way through the system, and ensure that the competencies are built into other key roles where people who use services require support.**

8.43 Individual budgets, in particular, could have a considerable impact on workforce roles and ways of working, and we expect to see growth in the numbers of personal assistants,

CASE STUDY

Integrated teams in Durham

People don't see their needs as neatly dividing into health problems and social care problems. They want a coherent response by public services. Recognising this, Sedgefield PCT, Sedgefield Borough Council and Durham County Council Social Services Department established the Sedgefield Adult Community Partnership in 2005.

Five integrated teams have been established across Sedgefield. The teams include district nurses, social workers and social work assistants, housing support officers, business support officers and occupational therapists.

Integrated working is proving much more efficient. For instance, having integrated teams allows staff to discuss housing options with people and prevent hospital discharge into unsuitable accommodation that will affect their health.

Use of the Single Assessment Process allows housing resources such as the Disabled Facilities Grant and money from the Housing Revenue Account to be targeted to prescribe technology to prevent falls, remind people to take medication, provide remote continuous assessment and even telemedicine.

Local people who use services were involved in designing how the partnership would work. An evaluation by Durham University has shown that people are impressed with the support they now receive.

employed directly by people who use services or their agents. A series of pilots managed by Skills for Care has begun to assess the nature of the personal assistant role, and this will also be explored through the individual budget pilots, seeking to devise and implement the best framework of training, support and regulation of this group of workers.

Working in the community

8.44 Both for the demonstration projects set out in Chapter 6, and for developing local care more broadly, we need to examine the workforce implications of receiving care closer to home and its associated regulations. A focus on care closer to home is likely to mean a different role for many specialist staff based in hospitals.

8.45 As care moves closer to people, many hospital-based staff will spend time working with multidisciplinary teams, with specialist nurses and with practitioners with special interests (PwSIs). There will be a need for full consultation with the staff affected by changing roles, and any new training needs will have to be appropriately addressed. Their role would be to provide oversight, training and patient consultations. **We would encourage all**

employers to use the job-planning process in the consultant contract, flexibilities in Agenda for Change and the incentives in new primary care contracts to facilitate the service changes laid out in this White Paper. New organisational or employment models that can be used by employers will be tested in the demonstrations described earlier and the Integrated Service Improvement Programme will provide a mechansim for sharing best practice.

Investing in our greatest resource

8.46 The NHS and social care sectors spend more than £5 billion annually on training and developing staff. Only a small fraction is targeted at staff working in support roles – the least qualified don't get the opportunity to participate in learning and development. None is spent in supporting informal carers. We will ensure the priorities of this White Paper are reflected in the way that money is spent.

8.47 In particular, we need to build up skills, especially in basic communication, in social care – where only 25 per cent of employees have a qualification. It is not acceptable that some of the most dependent people in our communities are cared for by the least well trained. We envisage a much greater role for informal carers and people who use services in training staff – with 'expert carers' running courses for nurses, doctors, allied health professionals, social workers and other care staff.

8.48 We will also continue to develop roles with greater responsibilities to encourage professional development. **We will encourage the development of these roles – such as advanced practitioners in imaging – where they can make most difference to delivery. We will also place an increased emphasis on PwSIs. To this end, we will develop and pilot new PwSI roles, including a PwSI for adolescent health (likely to be particularly focused on disabled children and the transitional period from teenager to adult) and a PwSI for learning disability.**

Harnessing available potential

8.49 We must ensure that our workforce has the capacity to meet people's needs. There are serious recruitment and retention problems to tackle in social care, where vacancy rates and turnover are often too high. **Under the joint Department for Education and Skills and Department of Health Options for Excellence Review, there will be nationally co-ordinated action to improve recruitment and retention in social care.**

8.50 Supplementing the Options for Excellence Review will be research the GSCC is undertaking into the professional role of social workers. Together, these will lead to proposals for developing the social work profession. Initial findings emphasise their core role in working in the context of ambiguity, uncertainty and risk, taking a holistic view of the lives of people who are often excluded or marginalised.

8.51 In the meantime, we will tap into the potential of groups of people who have, by and large, not been attracted into health and social care, and who have limited or no access to learning opportunities. We propose to extend recruitment to disadvantaged groups, young people, older people and volunteers, and people who have used services and can now make a new career in a caring role. The NHS Widening Participation in Learning programme and similar programmes in social care will be extended to support more diverse recruitment. We must also ensure that informal carers can move in and out of the paid workforce.

8.52 Health and social care organisations should also make good use of the many volunteers doing excellent work in the caring sector. To help with this, the Department of Health and the Home Office have funded a joint project led by Volunteering England to produce guidelines to encourage greater consistency in how volunteers are managed within the health service. This is scheduled for publication shortly.

8.53 Finally, we must ensure that health and social care employers are good employers. Evidence is growing that the highest-performing organisations have good employment practices. This includes local organisations fulfilling statutory duties on race, disability (from December 2006) and gender equality (from April 2007).

8.54 Yet, being a good employer is more than simply meeting legal requirements: supporting a good work–life balance, flexible working, childcare provision and healthy workplace policies are important to ensure that staff can perform to their full potential. **The Department of Health will work with the Department for Work and Pensions and the Health and Safety Executive to promote healthy workplaces in health and social care, and model employment practices that attract and retain the best staff with the best skills.**

References

1 www.childcarelink.gov.uk/index.asp

2 GMC consultation on revalidation, General Medical Council, 2000

3 Shipman Inquiry: Safeguarding patients – lessons from the past, proposals for the future, The Stationery Office, 2004

4 The Bichard Inquiry Report (HC 653), The Stationery Offfice, June 2004

5 A First Class Service: Quality in the new NHS, Department of Health, July 1998

6 An organisation with a memory, Department of Health, June 2000

CHAPTER 9

A timetable for action

Introduction

9.1 This document describes a comprehensive and integrated programme of reform for community health and social care. It sets out a long-term strategy that will put local people at the centre of local decision making. It signals a fundamental culture change and a shift in focus, backed up by a number of mechanisms and incentives to support delivery.

9.2 Our programme of reform includes a comprehensive set of actions which are identified in the preceding chapters **in bold**. This chapter spells out the timescale against which the central recommendations in each chapter will be taken forward. They, in turn, will support a programme of local action in the period to 2008/09.

9.3 The emphasis will be on making measurable progress in:
- promoting independence and well-being of individuals through better community health and social care and greater integration between local health and social care organisations;
- developing capacity through a wider range of service providers to secure value for money and improved access to community health and care services;
- changing the way the whole system works by giving the public greater control over their local services and shifting health services from acute hospitals into local communities.

9.4 To achieve this will require the full participation of a range of stakeholders, including local people, the third sector, the independent sector, Primary Care Trusts (PCTs), local authorities, and community health and social care professionals.

9.5 A small, central team will oversee implementation and will manage progress around several key themes. The central team will take ownership of a co-ordinated approach to implementation, tracking progress and ensuring delivery.

Key implementation tasks and timings by commitment

Chapter 2 – Enabling health, independence and well-being

Commitment	Key milestones
NHS 'Life Check'	• Develop on-line self-assessment – 2006/07 • Pilot NHS 'Life Check' in spearhead PCTs – 2007/08
Announcement on national demonstration sites for psychological therapies for mental health	• During 2006
Director of Adult Social Services (DASS)	• April 2006: new guidance issued to local authorities
Align budget cycles between health and local government	• 2007/08
New QOF measures for health	• 2008/09: New measures and well-being incorporated

Chapter 3 – Better access to general practice

Commitment	Key milestones
PCTs to take action on poor provision	• With immediate effect
PCTs invited to participate in national procurements	• Summer 2006
Guaranteed acceptance on an open list and streamlined registration rules	• Begin in 2007/08
Changes to 'closed list' rules	• Effects from 2007/08
Obligation on PCTs to provide detailed information on hours and services as well as new services	• Available in 2007/08
Review of PMS funding arrangements	• Report in early 2007
New Expanding Practice Allowance	• To be considered during 2006/07
PCTs offering more responsive opening hours	• 2007/08

Chapter 4 – Better access to community services

Commitment	Key milestones
Extend scope of direct payments	• As parliamentary time allows
Roll-out of individual budget pilots	• Impact immediate – 2006/07
National bowel screening programme	• End 2006
Development of an urgent care strategy	• End 2006
Improving choice and continuity in maternity services	• In place by 2009
End of campus provision for people with learning disabilities	• By 2010
End-of-life care networks	• In place by 2009

Chapter 5 – Support for people with longer-term needs

Commitment	Key milestones
Information prescription for all with long-term or social care needs	• By 2008
Establish an information service/ helpline for carers (or delegate to a voluntary organisation)	• By 2007/08
Short-term home-based respite support for carers in place	• Begin implementation in 2006, full implementation by 2007/08
Personal Health and Social Care Plans for those with both social care needs and a long-term condition	• In place by 2008
Joint networks and/or teams for management of health and social care needs between PCTs and local authorities	• Establish by 2008
Demonstration project to reduce A&E admissions on 1 million patients	• Project commences in 2006 • Share findings in 2008

Chapter 6 – Care closer to home

Commitment	Key milestones
Demonstration sites in six specialties to define appropriate models of care	• 2006/07 (time of study 12 months)
PCT local delivery plans not approved unless a clear strategy for shifting care is a major component	• Protocol in place by 2008
Establish an expert group on preventative health spending	• End 2006
Details on timing and tender process for new generation of community hospitals	• Summer 2006
PCTs demonstrate they have followed proper processes on future of community hospitals	• With immediate effect
New turnaround teams for service reconfiguration with focus on tackling causes for local imbalances	• Begin in 2006
Unbundle tariff	• From 2007/08
Extend to community setting	• 2007/08
Best practice tariff	• As early as possible

Chapter 7 – Ensuring our reforms put people in control

Commitment	Key milestones
Review of surveys to determine how to make them more effective in the future	• Autumn 2006
National commissioning framework	• First part in summer 2006, subsequent parts later in 2006
Develop 'local triggers' relating to public satisfaction and service quality	• Consult in spring 2006, guidance by autumn 2006
Establish social enterprise fund to provide support for third-sector suppliers wishing to enter the market	• Establish from April 2007
Review of Public and Patient Involvement	• By 2006

Revised commissioning assessment of PCTs and local authorities	• During 2006
Comprehensive single complaints system	• By 2009
Synchronise joint performance management systems	• By 2008

Chapter 8 – Making sure change happens

Commitment	Key milestones
Review provision of health and social care information	• End 2006
Information pilots – to determine how best to join up health and social care information	• Pilots to begin in 2006
Develop and pilot new practitioners with special interest roles	• 2007/08

The consultation and the listening exercise: the main messages

It was lovely after that first meeting to come back and say, 'Goodness! They've made all the changes we suggested!' ... We were cynical at first, saying 'As if they are going to listen to us,' but you really have.

MEMBER OF THE CITIZENS' ADVISORY PANEL

A.1 Genuinely patient-centred care can happen only if we listen to the people who use these services.

A.2 Society is changing and so too are people's needs. Our population is getting older, chronic conditions are increasing and becoming more complex, and we need to do more to prevent ill-health and support people to live as independently as possible. The importance of listening cannot be underestimated in facing these and other challenges.

A.3 In addition to the consultation on the adult social care Green Paper, *Independence, Well-being and Choice*, we undertook a major public engagement exercise to support the next stage of reform and improvement in NHS and social care. *Your health, your care, your say* comprised a series of four regional deliberative events accompanied by a range of local events and activities. Extra efforts were made to ensure that seldom-heard groups were included in the consultation. The process culminated

in a national event held in Birmingham, in which almost 1,000 people took part. A questionnaire was also available for people who wanted to have their say but were not involved in a deliberative event. Over 36,000 questionnaires were completed.

A.4 Participants in the regional and national events were randomly selected from the electoral register, up-weighted for disadvantaged groups. A recruitment questionnaire ensured that these participants were drawn from a range of social backgrounds and circumstances. The listening events were deliberative in nature, with a *Citizen's guide* given to participants beforehand to introduce the key issues in an informative and open manner.

A.5 A 'citizens' panel' provided independent, objective scrutiny and ensured that the consultation was citizen-led. The panel comprised 10 members of the public recruited to match the demographic profile of the delegates at the deliberative events. The youngest was 23 and the

oldest 82; one member was unemployed and others' occupations included a retired machine operator, an underwriter, a fashion designer and a gardener. Their advice on the language and format of the materials for the regional deliberative events was invaluable in making sure the text was straightforward and free of jargon. The role continued beyond the listening exercise; before this White Paper was published, they met with the Health Secretary and her ministerial team and acted as a sounding board for the policy themes and context.

A.6   In looking ahead to the next 15 to 20 years, we have paid attention to what people have told us is important to them. This is what they said.

Better health, independence and well-being

A.7   On adult social care services, people said we needed to do far more to increase independence and inclusion within local communities and to shift towards prevention and promoting well-being. They recognised the importance of services such as transport, housing, leisure and education in achieving this. There was strong support for the introduction of individual budgets to give people more choice and control. Many people, particularly those who currently receive services, also welcomed the opportunity to discuss the implications of supporting people who use services, their carers and the professionals who

support them to assess and manage risk in their daily lives, so that they can be more independent where that feels right to them.

A.8   In the *Your health, your care, your say* exercise there was a strong desire for more help to support people to maintain their independence and feel part of society, with more emphasis on tackling loneliness and isolation, especially for older people, vulnerable people and those caring for others.

A.9   Some 59 per cent of people told us that their health is very important to them but they could do more to be healthy. They recognise their own responsibility for this and want help in making healthy choices that build on the opportunities for healthy living set out in *Choosing Health*. People know that prevention is better than cure and believe it is more cost-effective for society because it reduces the risk of long-term illness and expensive treatments. They want support from health and social care to be healthy and to get on with their lives.

A.10   They would like the NHS to become a service with a focus on prevention rather than one that focuses predominantly on curing illness. Of nearly 1,000 participants at the national Citizens' Summit, 86 per cent thought professionals in their local GP practice should provide more support to help them manage their own health and well-being.

A.11 They want to see a wider range of professionals – particularly practice and community nurses and pharmacists – involved in health improvement, disease prevention and the promotion of independence. As with respondents to *Independence, Well-being and Choice*, they want to see more sustained and joint action across government and between local agencies, including education, housing, environment, transport and leisure services, to make this happen.

A.12 Some 61 per cent said that being given more information about their health and the services available to them locally would make a big difference. They particularly want to know more about the availability of social care services.

A.13 The public believes health checks could be cost-effective, if done in the right way. If they are more knowledgeable, they think this will enable earlier intervention and prevention of ill-health.

More responsive services with fast and convenient access

A.14 When they need to access services, people expect this to be quick and easy. They want services to fit the way they live their lives and they do not want to have to adjust their lives to fit around the way services are organised. A wider range of times when services are available is a priority. People want more information about

services: 50 per cent of respondents to the *Your health, your care, your say* consultation said this would make a big difference to them. Similar statements were strongly expressed during the consultation on *Independence, Well-being and Choice*.

A.15 There is a clear and strong desire for GP services to be open at more convenient times. People want to be able to get rapid access to care and to be able to book appointments in advance. They do not expect a 24/7 service, but they do want more flexibility around evening and early morning opening times during the week and Saturday morning openings.

A.16 People who care for others, as well as those with the greatest need for care, such as older people, people with a terminal illness, people with a mental illness and people with drug problems, think rapid access for them could help prevent their needs reaching crisis point. Most people think priority should be given to those with the greatest need and most at risk – inequalities remain and have to be tackled.

Better support for people with the greatest need to continue to live more independently

A.17 There is widespread support for improving services for people with ongoing needs to enable them to live more independently, with dignity and respect. People want services to support them to maintain their independence and social inclusion. They think this will help reduce their need for more expensive residential care and medical help in future. However, they recognise that residential and nursing care will continue to play a role in caring for and supporting some people with high levels of need.

A.18 People with ongoing needs want services that are joined up more effectively across organisations. They want services to be more focused on the totality of their needs, with a single case manager and an integrated assessment of their needs. A common complaint across health and social care services is that people who access services are assessed separately by multiple agencies and have to repeat the same information about themselves to every new professional they meet.

A.19 There is particular support for greater personalisation of services. Responses to *Independence, Well-being and Choice* widely welcomed extending the availability of direct payments and the introduction of individual budgets for people to stay as independent, active and in control of their own lives as their circumstances allow. There was also significant support for the wider use of self-assessment and more streamlined assessment processes, including the sharing of personal information between appropriate agencies to enable joined-up care.

More services available closer to home and in the community

A.20 In the consultation on *Independence, Well-being and Choice,* people were concerned about shortages in home care services, with many parts of the country experiencing staff shortages. People thought more emphasis should be placed on exploring the potential of assistive technologies to support people and their carers in their own homes. For example, passive movement sensors can detect if a person has fallen and trigger early help, or can detect if a person with dementia has left a safe environment and alert the carer. Technology can be used to monitor some long-term conditions, such as diabetes, in the home, and can help the individual retain more control over their health and condition.

A.21 People responding to *Your health, your care, your say* expressed an interest in new and innovative ways of providing hospital services, such as diagnostic tests and routine surgery, in community settings – provided these are safe and of high clinical quality, and do not result in changes to local hospitals that make it harder for people to get convenient access to emergency or more complex care.

A.22 Fifty-four per cent of people at the national Citizens' Summit positively supported moving hospital services to community settings. They were realistic – and initially cautious – that there were bound to be implications for general hospitals themselves. Provided that local people are properly engaged in decisions about shifting services, there was a majority view that the benefits of a managed shift were worthwhile.

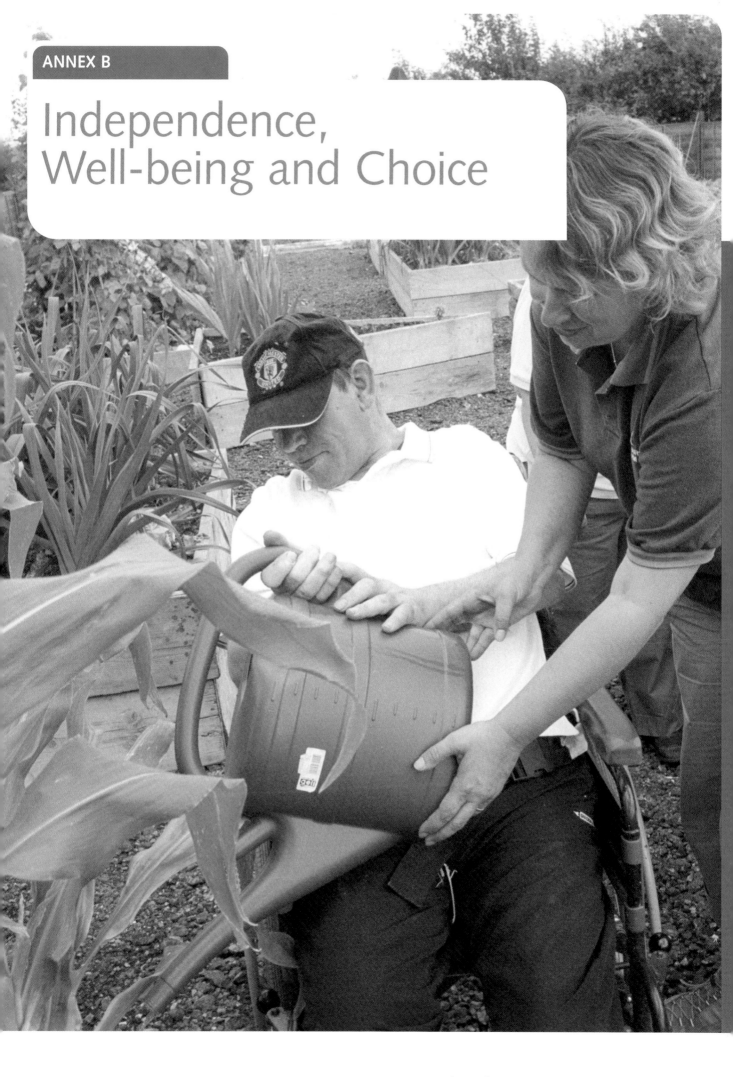

Independence, Well-being and Choice

Our vision for social care for adults in England

B.1   Our society is based on the belief that everyone has a contribution to make and has the right to control their own lives. This value drives our society and will also drive the way in which we provide social care.

B.2   This is a vision for all adults. It includes older people and younger adults who need care and support, people who are frail, people with a disability or mental health problems and people who care for or support other adults. It is also a vision for those who provide care services.

B.3   Services should be person-centred, seamless and proactive. They should support independence, not dependence and allow everyone to enjoy a good quality of life, including the ability to contribute fully to our communities. They should treat people with respect and dignity and support them in overcoming barriers to inclusion. They should be tailored to the religious, cultural and ethnic needs of individuals. They should focus on positive outcomes and well-being, and work proactively to include the most disadvantaged groups. We want to ensure that everyone, particularly people in the most excluded groups in our society, benefits from improvements in services.

B.4   Over the next 10 to 15 years, we want to work with people who use social care to help them transform their lives by:
- ensuring they have more control;
- giving them more choices and helping them decide how their needs can best be met;
- giving them the chance to do the things that other people take for granted;
- giving the best quality of support and protection to those with the highest levels of need.

B.5   We will achieve this by:
- changing the ways social care services are designed. We will give people more control over them through self-assessment and through planning and management of their own services;
- developing new and innovative ways of supporting individuals;
- building and harnessing the capacity of the whole community to make sure that everyone has access to the full range of universal services;
- improving the skills and status of the social care workforce.

B.6   In summary, the vision we have for social care services is one where:
- services help maintain the independence of the individual by giving them greater choice and control over the way in which their needs are met;

- the local authority and Director of Adult Social Services have key strategic and leadership roles and work with a range of partners, including Primary Care Trusts and the independent and voluntary sectors, to provide services which are well planned and integrated, make the most effective use of available resources, and meet the needs of a diverse community;
- local authorities give high priority to the inclusion of all sections of the community and other agencies, including the NHS, recognise their own contribution to this agenda;
- services are of high quality and delivered by a well-trained workforce or by informal and family carers who are themselves supported;
- we make better use of technology to support people and provide a wide range of supported housing options;
- we provide services with an emphasis on preventing problems and ensure that social care and the NHS work on a shared agenda to help maintain the independence of individuals;
- people with the highest needs receive the support and protection needed to ensure their own well-being and the safety of society;
- the risks of independence for individuals are shared with them and balanced openly against benefits.

B.7 We do not deliver this vision at the moment. Sadly, the organisation and provision of our services do not help everyone to meet these goals consistently.

B.8 We want to use this vision to demonstrate where we need to change and to guide the way we provide care. Our challenge is to make this vision a reality.

ANNEX C

Glossary

Acute care	Care for a disease or illness with rapid onset, severe symptoms and brief duration
Agenda for Change	The system of pay put in place in 2004 for most NHS-employed staff. Pay is linked to job content, and the skills and knowledge staff apply to perform jobs. The system is underpinned by a job evaluation scheme
Alternative Provider of Medical Services (APMS) contracts	This is one type of contract Primary Care Trusts (PCTs) can have with primary care providers. This contract is particularly designed to bring in new types of provision, such as social enterprise and the voluntary sector. See also **General Medical Services (GMS)** and **Personal Medical Services (PMS) contracts**
Assistive technology	See **Telecare**
Audit Commission	An independent body responsible for ensuring that public money is spent economically, efficiently and effectively in the areas of local government, housing, health, criminal justice and fire and rescue services
Balanced scorecard	A way of adding together measures of different aspects of an organisation's performance so that overall progress is clear, as is achievement of individual goals
Better Regulation Executive	A government body with responsibility for taking forward the Government's commitments to ensure regulation is necessary, the cost of administering regulation is reduced and inspection and enforcement regimes are rationalised in both the private and public sector
Care Services Improvement Partnership (CSIP)	The Care Services Improvement Partnership (CSIP), part of the Care Services Directorate at the Department of Health, was set up on 1 April 2005 to support positive changes in services and in the well-being of people with mental health problems, people with learning disabilities, people with physical disabilities, older people with health and social care needs, children and families with health and social care needs and people in the criminal justice system with health and social care needs

Child and adolescent mental health services (CAMHS)	Specific mental health services for children and young people
Children's Centres	Children's Centres are local facilities designed to help families with young children by providing access to a range of key services under one roof such as health, social care and parenting support
Children's Trusts	Children's Trusts are organisational arrangements which bring together strategic planners from relevant sectors to identify where children and young people need outcomes to be improved in a local area and to plan services accordingly
Choose and Book	Currently being introduced throughout England, Choose and Book is an NHS initiative that allows people to make their first outpatient appointment, after discussion with their GP, at a time, date and place that suits them
Choose and Book menu	The Choose and Book menu is the list of services available to be chosen by a patient following a search by a GP for a particular specialty or clinic
Choosing Health	A White Paper published on 16 November 2004 which set out proposals for supporting the public to make healthier and more informed choices in regard to their health
Citizens' Summit	The final stage in the *Your health, your care, your say* listening exercise which involved almost 1,000 people from across the country and from all walks of life discussing and agreeing priorities for community health and care services. They deliberated policy options and prioritised them, including options raised spontaneously by people in four previous regional events. See also **Your health, your care, your say**
Commission for Social Care Inspection (CSCI)	The single independent inspectorate for all social care services in England

Commissioning	The full set of activities that local authorities and Primary Care Trusts (PCTs) undertake to make sure that services funded by them, on behalf of the public, are used to meet the needs of the individual fairly, efficiently and effectively
Community care	Care or support provided by social services departments and the NHS to assist people in their day-to-day living
Community hospitals	Local hospitals serving relatively small populations (less than 100,000), providing a range of clinical services but not equipped to handle emergency admissions on a 24/7 basis
Community matrons	Community matrons are case managers with advanced level clinical skills and expertise in dealing with patients with complex long-term conditions and high intensity needs. This is a clinical role with responsibility for planning, managing, delivering and co-ordinating care for patients with highly complex needs living in their own homes and communities
Community strategies	Plans that promote the economic, environmental and social well-being of local areas by local authorities as required by the Local Government Act 2000
Continuing professional development (CPD)	The means by which professionals demonstrate to their professional body that they are updating and maintaining their skills
Crisis resolution teams	Teams providing intensive support for people with severe mental illness to help them through periods of crisis and breakdown
Direct payments	Payments given to individuals so that they can organise and pay for the social care services they need, rather than using the services offered by their local authority

Directgov	A website (www.directgov.uk) that provides a first stop for a wide range of information on national and local government and associated services, including education and learning, travel and transport and health and well-being
Directors of Adult Social Services (DASSs)	A statutory post in local government with responsibility for securing provision of social services to adults within the area
Directors of Public Health (DPHs)	A chief officer post in the NHS responsible for public health, Directors of Public Health (DPHs) monitor the health status of the community, identify health needs, develop programmes to reduce risk and screen for early disease, control communicable disease and promote health
Disabled Facilities Grants (DFG)	Grants issued by councils towards meeting the cost of providing adaptations and facilities (such as bath grab rails) to enable disabled people to continue to remain independent in their own homes
District general hospital (DGH)	A hospital which provides a range of clinical services sufficient to meet the needs of a defined population of about 150,000 or more for hospital care but not necessarily including highly specialised services
Expert Patient Programme (EPP)	The Expert Patient Programme (EPP) is an NHS programme designed to spread good self care and self-management skills to a wide range of people with long-term conditions. Using trained non-medical leaders as educators, it equips people with arthritis and other long-term conditions with the skills to manage their own conditions
Extended schools	Schools that provide a range of services and activities, often at times outside the normal school day, to help meet the needs of children, their families and the wider community. The Government wants all children to be able to access a core set of extended school services by 2010

Fair Access to Care Services (FACS)	Guidance issued by the Department of Health to local authorities about eligibility criteria for adult social care
Framework contract	A contract listing a range of suppliers who have demonstrated that they are able to supply specified goods or services. Once in place, the contract enables organisations to call upon one or more of the suppliers to supply the goods or services as they are required
General Medical Council (GMC)	The statutory body responsible for licensing doctors to practise medicine in the UK. It protects, promotes and maintains the health and safety of the public by ensuring proper standards in the practice of medicine
General Medical Services (GMS)	This is one type of contract Primary Care Trusts (PCTs) can have with primary care providers. It is a nationally negotiated contract that sets out the core range of services provided by family doctors (GPs) and their staff. See also **Alternative Provider of Medical Services (APMS) contracts** and **Personal Medical Services (PMS) contracts**
General Social Care Council (GSCC)	The social care workforce regulator. It registers social care workers and regulates their conduct, education and training
Gershon Review	An independent review of public sector efficiency commissioned by HM Treasury and conducted by Sir Peter Gershon. The report, *Releasing resources to the front line,* was published in July 2004 and was incorporated into the 2004 Spending Review. To support implementation, the Department of Health established the Care Services Efficiency Delivery programme
GPwSI	General Practitioners with Special Interests (GPwSI) supplement their generalist role by delivering a clinical service beyond the normal scope of general practice. They may undertake advanced procedures or develop specific services. They do not offer a full consultant service. See also **Practitioners with Special Interests (PwSI)**

Green Paper	A preliminary discussion or consultation document often issued by the government in advance of the formulation of policy
Health Direct Online	The Health Direct Online service is being developed to promote people's understanding of health and provide advice, information and practical support to encourage healthier ways of living that improve the quality of all our lives and communities
Health trainer	NHS-accredited staff who will help people in their community to make changes in their lifestyle in the interests of their health and well-being
Healthcare Commission	The independent inspectorate in England and Wales that promotes improvement in the quality of the NHS and independent health care
HealthSpace	A secure place on the internet (www.healthspace.nhs.uk) where people can store personal health information such as the medication they take and details of height and weight
Healthy Schools programme	A programme overseen by the Department of Health and the Department for Education and Skills, which encourages schools to contribute to the improvement of children's health and well-being. To become a Healthy School, schools must meet certain criteria in four core areas: personal, social and health education (PSHE), healthy eating, physical activity and emotional health and well-being
Improving the Life Chances of Disabled People	A report, published by the Prime Minister's Strategy Unit, which sets out a 20-year strategy focusing on independent living and enabling choice and control for disabled people
Independence, Well-being and Choice	*Independence, Well-being and Choice: Our Vision for the Future of Social Care for Adults in England* is a Green Paper setting out the Government's proposals for the future direction of social care for adults of all ages in England

Independent sector	An umbrella term for all non-NHS bodies delivering health care, including a wide range of private companies and voluntary organisations
Individual budgets	Individual budgets bring together a variety of income streams from different agencies to provide a sum for an individual, who has control over the way it is spent to meet his or her care needs
Integrated Service Improvement Programme (ISIP)	An NHS programme that integrates the planning and delivery of benefits from the investment in workforce reform, Connecting for Health and best practice from the Modernisation Agency and NHS Institute. The programme aims to drive delivery of efficiency through effective commissioning and integrated planning. The programme supports the delivery of savings as set out in Sir Peter Gershon's report on public service efficiencies to the Chancellor. See also **Gershon Review**
Kaiser Permanente	A US-based, not-for-profit, health care organisation, based in Oakland, California. It serves the health care needs of members in nine states and Washington, D.C.
Local Area Agreements (LAAs)	A Local Area Agreement (LAA) is a three-year agreement that sets out the priorities for a local area in certain policy fields as agreed between central government, represented by the Government Office, and a local area, represented by the local authority and Local Strategic Partnership (LSP) and other partners at local level. The agreement is made up of outcomes, indicators and targets aimed at delivering a better quality of life for people through improving performance on a range of national and local priorities
Local authority	Local authorities are democratically elected local bodies with responsibility for discharging a range of functions as set out in local government legislation

Local Delivery Plan (LDP)	A plan that every Primary Care Trust (PCT) prepares and agrees with its Strategic Health Authority (SHA) on how to invest its funds to meet its local and national targets, and improve services. It allows PCTs to plan and budget for delivery of services over a three-year period
Local Strategic Partnerships (LSPs)	LSPs bring together representatives of all the different sectors (public, private, voluntary and community) and thematic partnerships. They have responsibility for developing and delivering the Sustainable Community strategy and Local Area Agreement
Long-term conditions	Those conditions (for example, diabetes, asthma and arthritis) that cannot, at present, be cured but whose progress can be managed and influenced by medication and other therapies
Lyons Review	An independent inquiry by Sir Michael Lyons which is examining the future role and function of local government before making recommendations on funding reforms to inform the 2007 Comprehensive Spending Review
Mental health services	A range of specialist clinical and therapeutic interventions across mental health and social care provision, integrated across organisational boundaries
Minimum Practice Income Guarantee (MPIG)	The Minimum Practice Income Guarantee (MPIG) was introduced as part of the new General Medical Services contract (introduced from April 2004) to provide income protection to general practices moving from the previous contract to the new, to prevent a reduction in income. It applies to those practices which hold General Medical Services contracts. See **General Medical Services (GMS)**
National Institute for Health and Clinical Excellence (NICE)	The independent organisation responsible for providing national guidance on the promotion of good health and the prevention and treatment of ill-health

National Minimum Standards (NMS)	National Minimum Standards (NMS) are standards set by the Department of Health for a range of services, including care homes, domiciliary care agencies and adult placement schemes. The Commission for Social Care Inspection (CSCI) must consider the NMS in assessing social care providers' compliance with statutory regulations
National Service Framework (NSF)	Department of Health guidance that defines evidence-based standards and good practice in a clinical area or for a patient group. Examples include mental health, coronary heart disease and older people
NHS Connecting for Health	An agency of the Department of Health that delivers new, integrated IT systems and services to help modernise the NHS and ensure care is centred around the patient
NHS Direct	NHS Direct provides 24-hour access to health information and clinical advice, via telephone (0845 46 47 in England), as well as a website (NHS Direct Online www.nhsdirect.nhs.uk) and an interactive digital TV service (NHS Direct Interactive). A printed *NHS Direct Healthcare Guide* is also available
NHS Electronic Care Records (NHS Care Records Service)	The NHS Care Records Service (NHS CRS) is being developed to provide a secure, live, interactive NHS Care Record for every patient in England, which will be accessible to all health and care professionals, whichever NHS organisation they work in
NHS Employers	The employers' organisation for the NHS in England, giving employers throughout the NHS an independent voice on workforce and employment matters
NHS Foundation Trusts (FT)	NHS hospitals that are run as independent, public benefit corporations, controlled and run locally. Foundation Trusts have increased freedoms regarding their options for capital funding to invest in delivery of new services

NHS Improvement Plan	A Government plan, published in June 2004, that sets objectives for the NHS and related agencies
NHS Plan	A Government plan for the NHS, published in July 2000, that set out a 10-year programme of investment and reform for the NHS
NHS Walk-in Centres	NHS Walk-in Centres are centres staffed by nurses that offer fast and convenient access to treatment and information without needing an appointment
Office for Standards in Education (Ofsted)	The Office for Standards in Education (Ofsted) is the inspectorate for children and learners in England. It is their job to contribute to the provision of better education and care through effective inspection and regulation
Ongoing need	A defined health and care need that continues over time, although the intensity of care and support needed will fluctuate
Opportunity Age	Cross-government strategy, published by the Department for Work and Pensions on 24 March 2005. The strategy aims to improve older people's access to public services, and make it possible for them to exercise more choice, and promote independence, enabling more older people to remain in their own homes
Organisation for Economic Co-operation and Development (OECD)	An international organisation with a core membership of 30 countries which promotes democratic government and the market economy. It is best known for its publications on economic issues and its statistics
Overview and Scrutiny Committee (OSC)	A committee made up of local government councillors that offers a view on local NHS and social care matters

Partnerships for Older People Projects (POPPs)	A two-year programme of work led by the Department of Health with £60 millon ringfenced funding (£20 million in 2006/07 and £40 million in 2007/08) for local authority-based partnerships to lead pilot projects to develop innovative ways to help older people avoid emergency hospital attendance and live independently longer. The overall aim is to improve the health, well-being and independence of older people
Patients' Forums (or Patient and Public Involvement Forums)	Patient-led organisations, established by the NHS Reform and Healthcare Professions Act 2002, for every trust (including NHS Foundation Trusts) and Primary Care Trusts (PCTs). Their functions include monitoring the quality of services and seeking the views of patients and carers about those services
Payment by Results (PBR)	A scheme that sets fixed prices (a tariff) for clinical procedures and activity in the NHS whereby all trusts are paid the same for equivalent work. See also **Tariff** and **Tariff unbundling**
Personal Medical Services (PMS) contracts	This is one type of contract Primary Care Trusts (PCTs) can have with primary care providers. This contract is locally negotiated with practices. See also **General Medical Services (GMS)** and **Alternative Provider of Medical Services (APMS) contracts**
Practice Based Commissioning (PBC)	PBC gives GPs direct responsibility for managing the funds that the Primary Care Trust (PCT) has to pay for hospital and other care for the GP practice population
Practitioners with Special Interests (PwSI)	The term covering all primary care professionals working with an extended range of practice. A PwSI will specialise in a particular type of care in addition to their normal role, eg a PwSI in dermatology would see patients with more complex skin ailments. See also **GPwSI**
Primary care	The collective term for all services which are people's first point of contact with the NHS

Primary Care Trusts (PCTs)	Free-standing statutory NHS bodies with responsibility for delivering health care and health improvements to their local areas. They commission or directly provide a range of community health services as part of their functions
Public Service Agreement (PSA)	An agreement between each government department and HM Treasury which specifies how public funds will be used to ensure value for money
Quality and Outcomes Framework (QOF)	Part of the contract Primary Care Trusts (PCTs) have with GPs. It is nationally negotiated and rewards best practice and improving quality
Secondary care	The collective term for services to which a person is referred after first point of contact. Usually this refers to hospitals in the NHS offering specialised medical services and care (outpatient and inpatient services)
Secondary prevention	Secondary prevention aims to limit the progression and effect of a disease at as early a stage as possible. It includes further primary prevention
Single assessment process (SAP)	An overarching assessment of older people's care needs to which the different agencies providing care contribute
Skills for Care	Skills for Care is responsible for the strategic development of the adult social care workforce in England. It supports employers in improving standards of care through training and development, workforce planning and workforce intelligence. Alongside the new Children's Workforce Development Council, it is the English component of Skills for Care and Development, the UK-wide Sector Skills Council (SSC) for social care, children and young people
Skills for Health	Skills for Health is the Sector Skills Council (SSC) for the health sector in the UK, covering all roles and functions within the NHS and independent sectors. It helps the sector develop solutions that deliver a skilled and flexible workforce to improve health and health care

Social Care Institute for Excellence (SCIE)	The Social Care Institute for Excellence (SCIE) is an independent registered charity established in 2001 to develop and promote knowledge about good practice in social care
Social enterprise	Businesses involved in social enterprise have primarily social objectives. Their surpluses are reinvested principally in the business or community
Social exclusion	Social exclusion occurs when people or areas suffer from a combination of linked problems including unemployment, poor skills, low incomes, poor housing, high-crime environments, bad health and family breakdown. It involves exclusion from essential services or aspects of everyday life that most others take for granted
Social Exclusion Unit (SEU)	Part of the Office of the Deputy Prime Minister, the Social Exclusion Unit (SEU) provides advice and produces reports with recommendations on tackling specific social exclusion issues
Spearhead Primary Care Trusts	The 88 Primary Care Trusts (PCTs) (70 local authorities) in the areas with the worst health and deprivation in England
Step-down care	Part of intermediate care facilities that are outside acute hospitals, enabling people who strongly value their independence to leave acute hospital and get ready to return home
Step-up care	Part of intermediate care facilities that are outside acute hospitals, enabling people who strongly value their independence to receive more support than is available at home
Strategic Health Authority (SHA)	The local headquarters of the NHS, responsible for ensuring that national priorities are integrated into local plans and for ensuring that Primary Care Trusts (PCTs) are performing well. They are the link between the Department of Health and the NHS

Supporting People programme	A grant programme providing local housing-related support to services to help vulnerable people move into or stay independently in their homes
Sure Start	Sure Start is a government programme to achieve better outcomes for children and parents through increased availability to childcare, improved health and emotional development for young people, and better parental support
Tariff	A set price for each type of procedure carried out in the NHS, for example a hip replacement. See also **Payment by Results (PBR)** and **Tariff unbundling**
Tariff unbundling	Current tariffs include several stages of a procedure, for example the follow-up outpatient appointments after an operation as well as the operation itself. Unbundling breaks the tariff down to cover these constituent parts
Telecare	A combination of equipment, monitoring and response that can help individuals to remain independent at home. It can include basic community alarm services able to respond in an emergency and provide regular contact by telephone as well as detectors which detect factors such as falls, fire or gas and trigger a warning to a response centre. Telecare can work in a preventative or monitoring mode, for example, through monitoring signs, which can provide early warning of deterioration, prompting a response from family or professionals. Telecare can also provide safety and security by protecting against bogus callers and burglary
Third sector	Includes the full range of non-public, non-private organisations which are non-governmental and 'value-driven'; that is, motivated by the desire to further social, environmental or cultural objectives rather than to make a profit
Universal services	Services provided for the whole community, including education and health, housing, leisure facilities and transport

Valuing People Support Team	A Department of Health team working to improve services for people with learning disabilities through regional programmes of events, networks and support for groups and partnership boards. Its work is underpinned by national programmes designed to support local implementation
Voluntary and community sector	An 'umbrella term' referring to registered charities as well as non-charitable non-profit organisations, associations, self-help groups and community groups, for public or community benefit
Wanless report/ Wanless review	An evidence-based assessment of the long-term resource requirements for the NHS. Commissioned by HM Treasury and conducted by Derek Wanless, the report, *Securing Our Future Health: Taking a Long-Term View,* was published in April 2002
White Paper	Documents produced by the government setting out details of future policy on a particular subject
'Year of care' approach	Describes the ongoing care a person with a long-term condition should expect to receive in a year, including support for self-management, which can then be costed and commissioned. It involves individual patients through the care planning process, enabling them to exercise choice in the design of a package to meet their individual needs
Your health, your care, your say	The listening exercise with the public about what their priorities are for future health and social care services. It comprised four regional events, a range of local events and other activities including questionnaires. The process culminated in a national Citizens' Summit. The events were deliberative, with a *Citizens' guide* given to participants beforehand to introduce the key issues

Abbreviations and acronyms

A&E	Accident and Emergency
APMS	Alternative Provider of Medical Services
CAMHS	Child and adolescent mental health services
CCBT	Computerised cognitive behaviour therapy
CPD	Continuing professional development
CSCI	Commission for Social Care Inspection
CSIP	Care Services Improvement Partnership
DASS	Director of Adult Social Services
DfES	Department for Education and Skills
DFG	Disabled Facilities Grants
DGH	District general hospital
DH	Department of Health
DPH	Director of Public Health
DWP	Department for Work and Pensions
EPP	Expert Patient Programme
FACS	Fair Access to Care Services
FT	NHS Foundation Trust
GMC	General Medical Council
GMS	General Medical Services
GP	General Practitioner
GPwSI	General Practitioner with Special Interests
GSCC	General Social Care Council
HTCS	Hospital Travel Cost Scheme
ICAS	Independent Complaints Advocacy Service
IM&T	Information management and technology
ISIP	Integrated Service Improvement Programme
LAA	Local Area Agreement
LDP	Local Delivery Plan
LSP	Local Strategic Partnership
MPIG	Minimum Practice Income Guarantee

NICE	National Institute for Health and Clinical Excellence
NMS	National Minimum Standards
NSF	National Service Framework
ODPM	Office of the Deputy Prime Minister
OECD	Organisation for Economic Co-operation and Development
Ofsted	Office for Standards in Education
OGC	Office for Government Commerce
OSC	Overview and Scrutiny Committee
PALS	Patient Advice and Liaison Services
PBC	Practice Based Commissioning
PBR	Payment by Results
PCT	Primary Care Trust
PMS	Primary Medical Services contract
POPPs	Partnerships for Older People Projects
PSA	Public Service Agreement
PTS	Patient Transport Service
PwSI	Practitioner with Special Interests
QOF	Quality and Outcomes Framework
SAP	Single Assessment Process
SCIE	Social Care Institute for Excellence
SEU	Social Exclusion Unit
SHA	Strategic Health Authority
SHAPE	Strategic Health Asset Planning and Evaluation
YHYCYS	Your health, your care, your say

Printed in the UK for The Stationery Office Limited
on behalf of the Controller of Her Majesty's Stationery Office

167372   1/06   JW4524